AS INSIDE, SO OUTSIDE

AS ABOVE, SO BELOW

—⁓—

Reconciling Science and Spirituality through Consciousness

by Stephen Aronson

THE KARNAK
PRESS

As Inside, So Outside
As Above, So Below

Reconciling Science and Spirituality Through Consciousness

The author has made every effort to provide accurate Internet addresses in this work at the time of publication. Neither the publisher nor author assumes any responsibility for errors or changes to such addresses that occur after publication. Further, the publisher and author have no control over and do not assume responsibility for third-party websites or their content.

The photograph of Stephen Aronson that appears on the back cover was taken by his daughter Courtney Sparks.

The Cover Photo, The Isthmus of Corinth, Greece, 2012, Stephen Aronson

First Edition: Paperback October 2024
ISBN: 978-1-957278-11-7
Printed in the United States of America

THE KARNAK PRESS

Austin, Texas

Dedication

I dedicate this book to the man who both guided and modeled for me the method and practice of George I. Gurdjieff's Fourth Way over nearly forty years. Dr. Keith Buzzell was both my spiritual mentor and second father. His influence on my inner life and on the manner in which I have learned to share my impressions and experiences with others suffuses my thinking and writing.

Keith's prodigious intellectual drive to understand ever more and more about how universal forces, from the underlying quantum realm to the outer cosmos, to human psychology and physiology, actually work and integrate ... despite their incommensurable dimensions ... matched and inspired my own interests and search. His insistence on verification and a relentless search for truth at deeper and deeper levels set him apart from ordinary men. His character was sincere, honest, direct but always compassionate and open to new possibilities. He had a wonderful sense of humor. He exemplified the Sufi recommendation that when dealing with others, try always to neither humble nor distress.

Gurdjieff used the phrase "a remarkable man" to describe "a man who stands out from those around him by the resourcefulness of his mind, and who knows how to be restrained in the manifestations which proceed from his nature, at the same time conducting himself justly and tolerantly towards the weakness of others."*

In this sense also, Keith Buzzell was the most remarkable of men I have encountered. Over the course of four decades, I never saw him manifest in a manner which contradicted this description. He was, for me, a living example of the possibility of maturing into such a person and proof incarnate of the promise of Gurdjieff's method to help me accomplish this aim.

Dr. Buzzell is still vicariously available through his writings and video interviews at fifthpress.org., and Fifth Press, Salt Lake City, Utah.

I wish, dear Reader, that you could also have known him.

---

* *Meetings with Remarkable Men*, Dutton & Co, NY, 1963, p.31

As Inside, So Outside

As Above, So Below

—ᗰᐤ—

Reconciling Science and Spirituality through Consciousness

"The most beautiful thing we can experience is the mysterious. It is the source of all true art and science."

~ Albert Einstein

Above

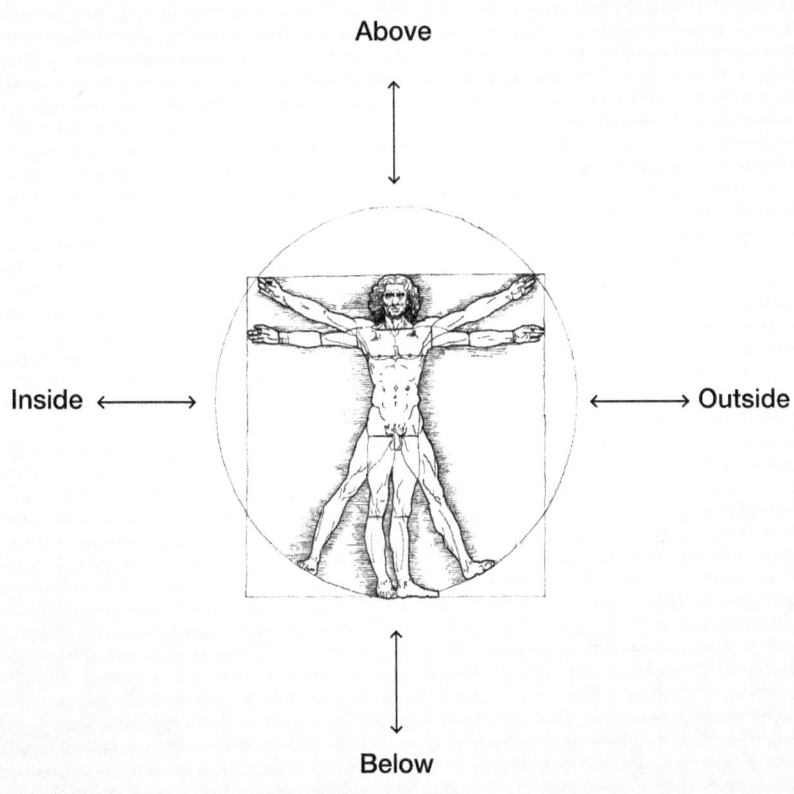

Inside ←→   ←→ Outside

Below

Contents

Foreword

If you think you are merely going to read an interesting collection of essays on questions related to Metaphysics, Psychotherapy, and Spiritual Search, you are quite mistaken.

So, a word of warning is in order.

To interact with Steve Aronson is never what one would conventionally expect.

This is something many of us have learned; some for several decades, others rather more recently. Actually, it is a feature often confirmed by persons who have had only a few minutes in his presence.

He rarely tells you, or writes about, what *he thinks* or merely *what he knows* regarding some issue. He *engages* you into a vivid experience of his inner world, and, with that passionate thirst for understanding one perceives in his eyes, or in his printed words, he seeks to enter your own inner world. He conveys an atmosphere of truth and simplicity which melts down any barriers or defense mechanisms which serve you in your dealings with the challenges of survival in ordinary existence. And what a respite one finds even in the briefest moments of such quality of communication.

One can always tell he is genuinely trying to learn from your experiences while he shares his experiences with you. He is one of those rare individuals who doesn't just wait for his turn to speak in the conversation. He listens, pure and simple. And, in resonance, you begin to listen with a depth unaccustomed in your experience.

When he asked me to write this foreword, I tried to plead my lack of literary, psychological, or philosophical credentials. But he was undaunted by my excuses.

Here is the nearest to credentials I could come up with:

When I first met Steve, I had a layman's knowledge of Existentialism and of the writings of Eric Fromm, Victor Frankl and Bertrand Russell.

To be frank, I had quite a high opinion of myself and of my approach to life, as was the case with my circle of "intellectual" and "artistic" friends. I supported all the right causes and had dropped out of Law in order to pursue my teaching vocation. I viewed myself as a supportive husband, an excellent father and a committed and creative schoolteacher, as well as a "serious" seeker of spiritual paths.

For many years, however, at the back of my mind there were flashes of suspicion that everything I had built was "on the surface of my being". I would sometimes become aware of traits in my personality that threatened my image of myself. My main source of anguish was that I was incapable of a true depth of authentic feeling. I would quickly suppress these thoughts, but they would keep popping up.

Now, at one level, externally, I am still the supportive husband, excellent father (and now also grandfather), committed and creative schoolteacher (now retired). I still support all the right causes and I try to be a sincere seeker in a spiritual path. But I no longer have a "high opinion" of what I used to call "myself". And I experience moments of true depths of feeling.

Steve Aronson played no small part in this process. Rest assured; he will play no small part in yours.

Federico Balsa,
Buenos Aires, Argentina
3/29/24

Quotations

"In the universe we live in, it is obvious that nothing is lost. Everything comes from somewhere and, having been changed or transformed to some degree, returns somewhere. Nothing which has taken form or is alive remains immutable and each of these changes serves life in some fashion. A human being cannot be an exception to this universal principle. Being endowed with thought, how can a man go through life without questioning himself and, being endowed with feeling, how can he remain indifferent to such questioning?"

Author unknown

"A human being is part of a whole, called by us Universe. A part limited in time and space, he experiences himself, his thoughts, and feelings as something separated from the rest ... a kind of optical delusion of his consciousness. The striving to free oneself from the confines of the ego, that moment of ecstasy, that experience of Eternity, right here is the one issue of true religion."

Einstein 1950

xi

Introduction

A connecting thread is woven through three seemingly separate levels of interlocking dimensions of existence into a pattern which we call The *Universe*: The *Macrocosmos* of Outer Space, the *Microcosmos* of Inner Space ... cells, molecules, atoms, subatomic particles ... and the third ... the *Non-Mass-Based Cosmos* of the *Human Mind* that can conceptualize and study the Cosmoses outside and within itself ... three worlds blended into One.

What possible reconciliation can there be regarding the incommensurable difference in size and time scale between galactic superclusters and their underlying foundation in the quantum realm of sub-atomic particles ... between galaxies and the atoms of which they are made ... between stars and the molecules which they produce when they explode... between planets and the lifeforms which are integrated onto and into them ... and between this human lifeform that we inhabit and the other forms of plant and animal life with which we are embedded?

These seemingly different realms, separated from each other by infinite orders of magnitude, have been explored by humans in different ways since our species appeared.

Until very recently, the data for such explorations came through the *experiences* of people, from their dreams, their epiphanies, their inspirations. These were transmitted as stories, creation myths, mythologies, and parables. These means of communicating perspectives which expand the capacity for understanding by using language to attempt to describe ineffable experiences through creating images in the mind of the listener. The visualizations and associations which appear when listening to a story can stimulate resonant emotions which give a richer, more nuanced feel when compared to intellectualized text alone and can illuminate a complex and subtle Whole which word alone cannot achieve.

With the advent of technology, we humans can now think our way into creating sensory augmenting instruments which can substitute for imagination so as to actually see, measure, manipulate, and even reach into these other two physical dimensions, the Macrocosmos and the Microcosmos, either to extract information, or in some cases, be able to manipulate them to have an effect in our surrounding material world. For example, bringing the process of nuclear fusion in stars onto the surface of our planet where it is not natural or modifying genetic material to alter the functioning of a human body by manipulating molecules are possibilities which did not exist before the technological advances of recent decades.

This capacity to test imagination against reality has led to enormous success in understanding how things work and eliminated the apparent need to invoke gods or mysterious "forces" as the explanation ... although giving names to the energies underlying existence ... such as *electromagnetism, gravity,* the *strong force,* the *weak force* or the *laws of nature* ... are still substitutes for the labels *Zeus, Apollo, Shiva, Brahma ... God.* Inexorably, we are rapidly enlarging our sense of the architecture of existence and the invisible forces that shape and maintain it while learning how these forces work and how to manipulate them to our advantage but we still don't understand why anything exists or why we are here to wonder about it.

My interest in the mystery of intuition, dreams, longings, epiphanies, and subjective experiences that cannot be explained by current scientific understandings has been pursued through the lens of my training as a psychologist and scientist by adhering to the scientific method of observation, experimentation, and confirmation. In this respect, I have tried to follow the guidance offered by G. I. Gurdjieff's admonition to never believe anything you hear or read from anybody unless you can confirm it for yourself through your own experience to your own satisfaction. This does not mean that what we hear and read may not be true. Some of it is true. Some of it is partially true. Some of it is not true at all. We have to take much information on face value because we ourselves cannot have a personal verification of the experience being pointed to such as the processes going on in the interior of a star or what it is like to live in a different culture if I have never done so. However, by looking to subjective experiences, we may discover very interesting correlations and possible confirmations with the deeper mysteries that are being explained to us, up to a point by modern science ... and, also, a new way to understand the symbolism of traditional religious expressions.

Interwoven Dimensions

From my perspective there are three *Facts* that call for an integrated understanding but so far have eluded such reconciliation. The first two facts are the very existence of the *Macrocosmos* of planets, stars, galaxies, and the existence of the foundational *Microcosmos* of atoms and subatomic particles. These have been repeatedly observed and theories about them confirmed. To date, both realms have been approachable through the scientific method of observation, theorizing, testing, confirmation ... as far as our instruments have been able to take us. However, they each appear to operate under different laws and are, as yet, unreconciled.

The remaining unreconciled and inexplicable *Fact* is the mystery of *Consciousness* itself, which seems far more elusive than the secrets of the other two dimensions... yet all appear to be intertwined at a deeper level.

The mystery of their inter-relationship demands recognition even if it cannot be explained by traditional "scientific" methodology. Throughout recorded history, cultures have shared their intuitions about the invisible world behind existence through creation stories, myths, parables, fairy tales. A symbolic rather than a literal examination of Western religion will often disclose the foundation of previous formulations. For example, the change from many impersonal gods to one supreme deity personally interested in each one of us ... still uses the concept of intelligent invisible powers underlying the mystery of existence with which one can communicate and have a relationship. The many saints and holy people prayed to in many religions can be seen as a transformation of the many "gods" viewpoint. Eastern religions may still be closer to their ancient roots and less trapped in literalism.

It is also a fact that modern sciences, particularly cosmology and quantum physics, are making discoveries that often echo the theories and inspirations conjured in the distant past, suggesting a confirmation rather than a discovery. It is also a fact that these discoveries and rediscoveries, these inspirations, dreams and epiphanies, all appear in the sphere of conscious awareness occupied by the receiver of the impression. History is full of stories of great scientists making their breakthrough recognitions in dreams, in thought-experiments, in Eureka moments. We have even less understanding of the fact of Consciousness than we do of the rest of the Universe. And yet, the secrets of the Universe occasionally appear in symbolic forms, images, hunches, or insights in the minds of humans, ordinary people as well as saints and scientists.

A current conundrum facing modern cosmology rests on the apparent fact that the Newtonian laws which successfully predict the movements of mass-based objects in Space-Time do not seem to apply to the quantum dimension of atoms and their sub-atomic constituents. Two different Cosmoses, the small nested within and as the foundation of the large, seem to operate under different rules. It seems reasonable to assume that the "laws" of the Psyche are not the same as the laws governing the material Universe, either. If anything, they appear to reflect aspects of the Quantum dimension.

Cosmos and Consciousness

So how can both the *Macrocosmos* which surrounds us and the *Microcosmos* within us be understood? Where is this understanding to take place and through what instrument? From what perspective do we study anything except through the sphere of our conscious awareness? And what do we use as an instrument in that study ... other than our *Attention*? Were it not for the sphere of our awareness, there would be nobody to notice and wonder about the cosmos outside or the cosmos inside. Within this zone of fluctuating subjective sensitivity are accumulated all our experiences with outer life and the *internal* reaction patterns programmed into a responsive dance with life ... along with our personal story and labels of who we are and what we have come to believe about our nature and role on this planet we have named "Earth".

Yet we also seem to have a different life inside of this Space of Awareness. How is it that there occasionally appears within our consciousness, access to information or perspectives or understandings that do not come transmitted through our external senses? It is in the Cosmos of our Psychological World and through the willed efforts of our psyche to utilize the attention available to it as an instrument of exploration, that we can investigate the Macrocosmos and the Microcosmos through the connecting space of the Third Cosmos of ourselves which both encompasses and is encompassed by the other two.

In this sense, the Universe appears to be an interlocking structure of at least three levels or distinct qualities. There are still many great mysteries attached to the Macro and Microcosmoses. For example, "where did all the materiality originate from?" ... "where is it all going ... and what, if ... anything, does it all mean?" The third great mystery is ... *Myself* ... and you, also dear ... Reader. It is the *Fact of Consciousness,* the Consciousness inside us all, the Consciousness that conceives and explores

4

the outer and inner dimensions. It is the Consciousness that can study Itself.

I have been very interested in the correlations between ancient wisdom and the discoveries of current science and, in particular, understanding how the structure of our psychology is integrated into the worlds above and the worlds below our apparent location in the scale of existence. My personal approach has been to bring the skepticism of the scientific method, as I understand it, to join with my developed capacity to be open to the deeper regions of my psychology and allow the two to blend while I watch what emerges from the darkness for the viewing of my inner eye.

The following essays are my attempt to explore this interrelationship in a style that works for me. I have chosen to write, not in traditional academic format with many references and footnotes ... there is much literature on this topic using that approach. My interest is in the open-ended exploration afforded by dialogue, the sharing of impressions without the pressure to come to conclusions, so as to open up the mind to *experience*, to *taste*, the profound mystery confronting us, a mystery that deepens when we include the phenomenon of Consciousness in the equation.

Outside of my area of psychological training, I am not an expert in physics, cosmology, biology, or the other hard sciences. I only have a long-ago Bachelor of Science and a lifetime interest in reading this material. My source for pondering these questions comes from combining my having learned a lot about a little ... along with a little about a lot ... with years of studying the inner workings of my mind ... and learning to pay attention to the creative impulse weaving tapestries of ideas and images through its mysterious interior.

It is because of my wish to reconcile two traditional pathways of search ... which I alternately call "Cosmos" and "Consciousness" or "Science" and "Spirituality" or "Rationality" and "Intuition" ... I offer these personal reflections on the inter-weaving relationship between our mysterious subjective experiences and the world of our ordinary sensorial, materialistic vision of life. These I share with you, dear Reader, to add my small contribution to these eternal questions.

As Inside, So Outside; As Above, So Below

Quotations

"The art and science of asking questions is the source of all knowledge."

Thomas Berger

"The key to creativity is to begin with an idea and then to let the muse take over."

Albert Einstein

"Discovery comes from seeing what everyone has seen and thinking what nobody has thought."

Jonathan Swift

7

As Inside, So Outside; As Above, So Below

Question

A question is a disturbance in the foundation of the "Known" …
a recognition of something missing,
something more,
something new …
unexpected. .

The current "Known" fractures.
A light shines through the rupture.
There is something else, something more, on the other side
that I did not realize.
What is it?

A question is an opening,
a wormhole,
suddenly connecting the past,
through the present,
with a new future possibility.

I have begun a journey,
a search for an answer to the question.
A relationship has appeared
between the question…
and a new future.

When I, myself, am in Question,
I become both the question and the seeker,
and I enter the realm of Question
as the sought for answer.

If a question carries more than idle curiosity, it energizes. The emotional energy we call "interest" can redirect Attention, change motivation, alter one's course ... both outside and inside.

Search outside requires the body. Search inside is a different dimension. Here, the body plays a useful role in providing a backdrop of sensation to facilitate an awareness of myself as a conscious *something* inside the body.

To be in Question is a quality of State ...a container which can hold our interest ... our energy ... and in which questions are born:

What am I?
What is my purpose?
Why do I exist?
Do I have meaning?
What do I question about myself?
What does it mean that I do not know myself?
How can there be more of me to discover than I currently know?
Am I a larger space that I am unfamiliar with?

Perhaps I only know myself in relation to what I am aware of in the proximity of the space of my subjective world. If so, then when I expand my attention into new areas of inner exploration, I am exploring more of myself. But ... what is this *myself* ...is it the part of me that believes it already knows itself ...or is it the whole of me not yet known ... how much remains to be known?

Each time I expand, each time I deepen my recognition of aspects I had not been aware of, each time I connect dots into patterns I had not noticed ... into what is my awareness and understanding expanding?

These questions remind me of the same questions currently asked by cosmologists and quantum physicists. *What is the Universe? What is it expanding into?*

No matter how far out we look towards the moment of Creation, nor how deep within the microscopic worlds we probe, there is still more ...always more...

We use specialized instruments, to extend our senses to explore the depths of space and the world of sub-atomic particles ...but ...*what* is asking the driving question which then demands the making of instrumental aids to help with the search into the unknown for the answer to the question which had appeared in a mind and stimulated a heart?

What instrument do I use to explore the ever-expanding depths of my psychological structure and potential? The instrument of Mind uses the tool of *Attention*, powered and directed by an emotional *Wish* to know… and the mysterious and elusive *Will* to pursue.

As with exploration of what lies both Above and Below …my Mind is the instrument I use in the search within, my inner telescope, my inner microscope, my inner seismometer.

This Mind watches mental activity while it is informed, by sensations, of the state of the body, and feels the flowing world of emotions, wishes, fears, hopes. This instrument must be trained, upgraded, matured, to make the search. It is developed and refined both through the process of making the search and through what the search discloses.

Where is the direction we call *Within*? I am directing my Mind to explore the depths *within* … itself! If I am *directing* my Mind … am I something different from my Mind?

All this from a question … a yearning to understand … that begins when a child first asks,

> *"Why is the sky blue?"*
> *"Where did I come from?"*
> *"Where do we go when we die?"*

As Inside, So Outside; As Above, So Below

Epiphany at the Synapse

L ate one night, in 1982, I was visiting with the man who would become my spiritual mentor, Dr. Keith Buzzell, in his eighteenth-cen-
tury farmhouse, deep in the forest of Western Maine. He was talking
about the phenomenon of neural transmission. I was on my feet, struggling to stay awake at 1 a.m., not wanting to leave his company until he
was ready to stop. The discovery of Gurdjieff's ideas, and Keith's connection with them, had appeared in miraculous fashion for me only a few
months earlier. Both the ideas and his understanding of them were manna
from Heaven for my parched and starving Essence.

Since my youth, I had been oriented to confirm for myself the truth of
a Reality 'behind reality.' Given my intellectual predilections, I was attracted to the path of scientific discovery – or rather, the continually expanding edge of what was 'known'. It seemed that what I was searching
for must lie in the darkness just beyond this always expanding circle of
light. Confronting the abyss at the terminus of the Known was
electrifying. I also was aware that the depth of my longing to confirm the
existence of this suspected underlying Reality made me vulnerable to
suggestibility, so I relied on my intellectual mind, as I understood it at
that time, and avoided trusting my feelings. As a result, even when faced
with inexplicable experiences, my *"formatory"* mind would intervene
and tell me that since my experiences were 'subjective', I therefore could
not use them for verification. ("formatory": Gurdjieff's term for the me-
chanical/associative/data-filled "machine" in, what he called our *"intellectual center"*.)

Then, one night, at age 39, a strange occurrence happened that I can
only describe as the most transformative 'vision' I have ever experienced,
the details of which I have explored in my book *"The Search for Meaning
and the Mystery of Consciousness"* under the heading "The Call". This
experience led me, within two weeks, to the discovery of the Gurdjieff
Work, of which I had been totally unaware. I knew immediately that *I had*

come home and my formatory logic surrendered to the emotional truth of the situation. Shortly thereafter, I made contact with Keith and entered a relationship which lasted nearly four decades until his recent passing.

So, long ago, there he and I were, in the wee hours of the morning, in the stillness of the forest, exploring what was currently known about the flow of electricity in the brain. Keith was speaking about the process of a 'something' moving along the axon to flip sodium-potassium ions back and forth across the membrane, producing an ionic-wave which, if sufficiently strong when entering the neuron body, would jump across the synapse to initiate another movement of the "something" along the next axon. The factual materiality of this process was so incomprehensibly complex ... and *intelligent* ... that I saw it could in no way be 'accidental.' There was an emotional excitement in my chest, and something began to shift. As he spoke, I was aware of my body struggling to stay awake and the effort of Will to command it to do so. At the same time, I was following a picture in my mind of the traveling "nerve impulse." My mind focused on the synapse between two nerve cells.

Then I saw it! There, in the *empty* space between the dendrites of one cell and the neighboring axon of the next cell, was proof my intellect had been unable to see despite all its opportunities to do so. The space was 'empty.' There was no structure. Nothing was there ... but *Everything* was there! Nothing could happen without including the *space*. The mystery of the laws and principles that underlay everything, was in the middle, in the center, in the space between things. The source of everything was in the 'Nothing.'

A tear rolled down my cheek. "Why am I crying," I asked Keith. He looked at me with understanding and replied, "The Truth is like that." In that moment I understood the *feel* and *taste* of Truth ... a particular resonance ... and I recognized that I could trust my intellect, avoid suggestibility, and know ... without *thinking thoughts.*

Subsequent Reflection

As time passed, I discovered a more nuanced understanding of what had happened at that transformational moment.

I had been looking, inside my mind, at a movie, a series of images forming in resonance with Keith's verbal description of the neural process. I was the *audience* for the movie. At the point in the "film" where neurotransmitter molecules detach from the dendrite of one nerve body to float into the synapse to establish communication with the next neuron axon in the chain ... an insight appeared ... an instantaneous understanding of the significance of the seemingly empty space between everything.

From where inside our minds do we view the 'movies' we call thoughts, daydreams, or experience "hunches", occurring in other parts of our brain? From where inside our minds do we view and experience the movie we call life? From where do we make the interpretations of the meanings of these movies which then frame and determine our lives?

At the moment of epiphany ... I ... represented by my understanding ... was floating in a state of bafflement, trying to comprehend the complexity of this naturally occurring process which underlies all life ... a process which connects the outer world of physical reality with the subjective, experiential inner world of a creature's sensitivity and thus, making possible communication between the two levels.

Then I saw that *something* ... inside the creature ... inside *myself* ... was *aware* of, processing and interpreting this information coming in from outside through neural transmission. The purpose of the transmission was to connect the creature with the world around it. The more neurons connected, the larger the "field" of awareness. The awareness itself was, either the combined product of all this electrical activity ... or ... all this electrical activity facilitated the quality of awareness to appear. ... or both.

Electro-magnetism is currently understood to be one of the four fundamental forces maintaining the Universe. That suggests to me that Awareness itself is related to the essential laws of the Universe, from the macro to the micro levels.

From my experience, Gurdjieff embeds this understanding in his recognition that nothing new appears without the interaction of three forces: something initiating, something being acted upon and a third variable which, if present, facilitates a blending of the first two into something new. In human life, this third factor may be new knowledge, a change in perspective, a shift in attitude, an alteration in understanding or a spontaneous creative impulse... which modifies a situation, opens a new possibility that was not present a moment before and could not appear within the confines of the previous viewpoint.

This third factor, if it appears, does so from a level *above* ... which allows for a new possibility. This *space of possibility* provides a new home for the other two factors which can find a different way of relationship.

If my mind is dense and full of strongly held beliefs, where will potential new ideas find a space in which to germinate? An open mind has a different configuration ... and potential ... than a closed mind.

In Gurdjieff's state of "Self-Remembering" ... which in my experience can, in one respect, be described as ... *being aware of oneself being aware of observing one's mental, emotional, and physical manifestations* ... the taste of the moment often carries the impression of awareness being in a "third location" observing the interaction between the inner world of thought, feeling and sensation, with the outer life around it. At the end of his last written work, *Life is Real Only Then When I Am*, Gurdjieff spoke about the "Third World of Man" possible from transformational inner work.

Philosophy and Science have long been aware of the mysterious void underlying our lives as reflected in questions such as, "Where was I before my conception? Where do I go when asleep or in a coma? Can anything of "me" survive the death of my body? Where does an epiphany reside prior to its appearance in my mind? When sub-atomic particles "pop into and out of existence", from where do they come and where do they go? Where did the Universe come from ... where was it before it ... was?

A new question eventually appeared: "How closely are Consciousness and Attention related to this mysterious void ... the space of nothingness between everything?"

As years passed, my attraction to the mystery and critical nature of the invisible ... invisible to our senses, but not our *intuition* ... component of existence has been a quasar on the horizon of my search.

These recognitions unfolded over many years of self-observation but all began that moment, late at night, in the depths of the Maine forest, while visualizing the flow of ions across the cell membrane of a single, imagined neuron. All that was to come was embedded, like a tree within a seed, in that instant of the taste of Truth.*

---

* Parts of this essay appeared as Preface to *The Third Striving*, Keith Buzzell, Fifth Press, Salt Lake, Utah, 2014

Pondering The Location of the Mind

I pause at the beginning of writing this piece to look out the window. I realize it has been over forty years since that fateful evening back in 1982 when I had my transformational encounter with the reality of the Synapse. These questions about the nature of mind have haunted me since. I decided the time had come, after four decades of "long pondering" this and related themes, to probe my mind for personally acquired information and experiences around this vexing mystery.

I refocus my attention on how the pine forest beyond is making a visual impression in my brain for my mind to experience. It looks to be outside my body, outside the house, although intellectually I have read that the light rays reflecting off the tree have entered my brain through my retinas (actually … extensions of my brain projecting to the surface) and traveled the optic nerve running from my eyes to the visual-processing part of my brain so that everything I can experience about the trees will actually be experienced in my brain for my mind to experience … like the patron at a show.

Now, I direct my attention to an evening star. On one level, I have read that the photons of distant galaxies may have left their stars millions of years before humans appeared on Earth … and in the farthest sources, billions of years before the Earth came into existence.

Yet, from another perspective, the star light is only entering me because I opened my eyes to it … and it is inducing resonances in my thoughts and feelings because I am attitudinally and emotionally open to it in the necessary way. As I reflect further, I realize that the degree of my noticing and openness depends on the *quality of my awareness* in that moment. When the starlight fills my awareness… physically… emotionally… and intellectually…has the time and distance between the star and my mind collapsed? Are we … for a moment … occupying the same "space" … somehow entangled?

The type of person we are and how our individual psychology is structured determine the state of mind that greets the light of a star. In a way, my mind has attitudinally reached out to the star and is sharing in the light of its sphere of influence in that moment. There is, for a brief instant, a relationship, an overlap, an interpenetration between my mind and the star. When starlight enters my eyes and is experienced through the appropriate state of consciousness, my mind expands to encompass the deeper experience.

Some people have no interest in stars, may know nothing about them, may not even look up on a starry night, may not even be able to see them in the polluted skies over their homes. In contrast, I once heard of a woman in rural Maine who was afraid to go out after dark because the reality of the stars in the pitch-black night sky terrified her. The psychological/ emotional /spiritual development of such people is different from that of stargazers and mystics ... so their minds will have different experiences.

The conception of a new impression is aptly named. The light enters my brain like a seed carrying potential information and insight. If it finds a fertile reception in the mind, something new is conceived. If of sufficient strength, it may then be birthed into manifestation with a power of its own.

What is true for my relationship with a star is true for my relationship with anybody and everything.

As I sit in my quiet office right now pondering these questions, I close my eyes and place attention into the sensation of my body. I send an intention to my muscles to relax ... and they do.

Now I am noticing my breathing and the music I set to play in the background to facilitate the emotional state that helps me to think and write about these types of questions ... now I am also aware of the ticking of the pendulum clock nearby. I am also cognizant of myself watching, from inside my mind, to see what, if any, thoughts arise. .... I also am aware of a wish for there to be no thoughts. Actually... sometimes ... my mind is acutely cognizant of moments without words or ideas ... just awareness of my body and the sound and feel of my surroundings. So ... my mind clearly encompasses much more than thinking. Then, there are the moments when I become aware of being aware of myself watching the content of my mind. This feels to be a level above my ordinary perceptions.

Try this for yourself, dear Reader. Take a few minutes. Can you find this quality of quiet and stillness in your own mind?

As I ponder over what I have just written, I notice the strangeness of the phrasing "watching the content of my mind". Everyone has some quality of this experience, starting at the limited low end of the range from what we ordinarily call "self-conscious embarrassment" ... to having conversations in my head ... to daydreaming ... to the extraordinary state of being-aware of myself as something separate from the content of my thoughts, my fantasies, or reactions. Our daily experience tells us that there is something that can see, hear, sense, and feel, gather information and impressions, and interact with phenomena in the inner world of our psychological makeup. We generally think about this something as ... "me" ... or "my mind". But... where is my mind located?

We all know where *the brain* is located ... but what is the location of my *mind*? Because we associate mind with thoughts, we assume mind resides only within the brain in our head along with our thinking.

But isn't my mind also aware of sensation, a pain in my left foot or an itch on my shoulder or hunger in my stomach or a warm relaxing feeling through my body? When my mind becomes aware of feelings of tenderness, or reverence, of surprise or concern ... or a desire... from *where* am I experiencing *those* phenomena?

Research has found a number of brain areas associated with feelings, judgments, perhaps even an area related to a subjective sense of self and others to a sense of spirituality. Since many of the phenomena in these different areas can be experienced simultaneously ... while one is also aware of directing the looking and searching for patterns, new information ... this begs the question as to the "location" of *that which can observe from beyond the conditioning.*

Contemporary science believes that all awareness is located only in our brain. For example, when I am having the experience of sensing my foot, although it feels like my attention has reached down my leg into my toes, the current neurological understanding is that my conscious attention has moved, not into my toes, but only into the location in the *cortical motor center of the brain*, which sends and receives signals from my foot. Establishing a conscious presence in this brain location, I can now be aware of signals coming from the other end of my body to which I was oblivious a moment prior.

From this perspective, everything that we 'experience' in the physical world around us is said to actually be seen, heard, tasted, smelled, felt and experienced inside the processing brain. Except ... that doesn't address the issue of how these sensory impressions are being *experienced* ... or *what* is experiencing them.

I now turn my attention to the clock on the wall. The sound of the clock enters my mind from the outside and is met with pre-programmed responses, understandings and labels stored inside from past experiences with clocks ... and time...from the *muscle memory* of winding pendulum clocks to the *emotional memory* associated with my grandparents' cuckoo clock. These, along with images and moving memories, must be *stored, in fragments*, throughout my entire brain, retrieved and recombined into a whole. Even when I listen to something as simple as the sound of a clock, the sound must be lighting up many areas of my brain simultaneously.

I wonder ... my senses tell me that the ticking clock exists outside my body. I see and hear it off to my left from where I am sitting in this room. My mind contains the information and experiences of my senses ... as well as my thoughts, reactions, opinions ... those from my past recollections to my future projections as well as my experience in the moment. Actually... my experience in the moment is organized by my past experiences and interpretations as well as my future expectations, hopes and concerns. This sounds ... and feels ... like my awareness has expanded into a huge library of associations unbound by time. If my attention has directed itself into the location, in my brain, where body and emotional memory are carried along the internet of neurons, why not assume that attention also flows down into and throughout the nerve cells entering and leaving the brain from the entire body? If my awareness in my brain is sensing the interior of my left foot, then the energy of Attention has expanded into the neural network, into the stream of information from my foot. *Experientially* ... it is inside my foot.

Attention can travel far beyond awareness of the interior of my body. Through my ears it can expand "as far as sound will carry". With my eyes, it expands "as far as the eye can see". When I "feel" another person's pain or joy, "my heart has reached out to them". Compassion is a blending of feeling and experience with another.

And ... my mind can do something that my body cannot. While my body is confined to the three dimensions of height, width and depth, my mind is not. *My mind can travel in time*. It can take me into my past to re-view, re-live, re-experience events. It can take me into the future, both near and far, to play out different possibilities and plan for different eventualities that have not yet happened. My mind can travel to imaginary worlds that cannot exist in three-dimensional space. It can enter into the psychological/ emotional realm of others to give me a taste of what they are experiencing in their inner world. The range of Mind seems to far exceed the parameters of the brain, reaching through time and dimensions.

So ... if when sensing my body I expand the sphere of my Attention into different sensory-motor brain areas ... creating the impression of expanding awareness into my body ... then where in my brain do I send my attention when time traveling ... or daydreaming ... or being aware of directing my awareness to simultaneously attend to the interaction between my inner and outer worlds in a given moment? Current neurological understanding suggests that attention has been directed from my frontal lobes into the memory storage areas of my brain, which then reach out to images in the visual center, words in the auditory center, memory of smell in the olfactory center and all other storage areas needed for the reminiscence or fantasy. These fragments must then be continuously blended into a recognizable whole at a speed so fast that I do not perceive the process, only the result.

I am aware that most of these mind phenomena seem to happen without my initiation but I can be aware that they are occurring. I can watch them and be interested to see what I can learn about "myself". But sometimes I *choose* to make the effort to "expand" my mind in this way. How do I *do that?* This neurological viewpoint seems to imply that what I call my "Mind" is limited to the circle of attention at a given moment and does not include brain activity that is "out of mind" or "unconscious" or "subconscious".

Dear Reader, why don't you try this yourself? Close your eyes. Sense and relax your body. Take yourself into your past and walk around for a while. Then imagine the future ... what do you find there? If you are relaxed and have your eyes closed, there are no outside stimuli causing your mind to leave the present moment. How did you *do* that?

From where "in my mind" am I observing and making these efforts? If I am my mind, how am I expanding myself? If I am something inside my mind, then what am I in relation to that mind?

The issue has grown in complexity since Descartes observed, "I think, therefore I am".

So ... as I quietly sit here in my relaxed body, breathing slowly, watching what is happening in my "mind", where do I locate this place of watching? If you are also trying this dear Reader, where do you locate yourself as the "Observer" of your mind's contents?

Our language tells us that we intuit a deeper reality than our rational thinking may be aware of. What do we mean when we say things like, ... "Are you out of your mind?" or "I wasn't in my right mind when I said that" or "I think I'm losing my mind"?

Am I something different from what I have always thought of as "my mind"? If I can lose my mind ... then what am I ... when separated from my mind? Is this a *different part of my mind* which is not typically available to me ... or perhaps I am not typically available to it? If I sometimes "don't know my own mind" ... or ... "I can't make up my mind" ... then my awareness would seem to be something which interacts with the arena called mind. Is "mind" a field phenomenon in which my awareness fluctuates?

In such a state I may even briefly lose track of my physical surroundings and not hear my name called. "Where were you?" I might be asked. "I don't know", I might reply. "My mind was somewhere else" ... *Somewhere* else? Where would my mind go when it goes "somewhere else?" Where has my attention gone ... and kidnapped "me" with it?

And while we are exploring these strange implications embedded in our language ... what does the term, to *expand* one's mind, mean? Our language talks about *closed* minds and *open* minds, *deep* minds, and *shallow* minds, *broad* minds, and *narrow* minds, *educated* minds and *ignorant* minds which hold little. We talk *about changing our mind.*

The Space of the Synapse

I am reflecting now on that astounding moment, many years ago, when I recognized the metaphysical implications of the *synapse* ... the space between the dendrites of a neuron and the axons of related neurons. As the electrical impulse flows through a neuron body, it reaches, at the tip of its forest of dendrites, a space separating them from the possibilities of communicating with surrounding neurons. The chain is broken. Neurons don't touch each other. They are all separated by a space.

We now know that many different forms of molecular structures are produced in the dendrites when sufficiently stimulated by the oncoming electrical current. Each type of neuro-transmitter molecule, each category with its own distinctive shape, is released in differing proportions and must "float" across the chasm (from its relativistic frame point) and find the precisely shaped "dock" on another neuron's receiving axon to "fit" as a key into its lock. When the combinations of locks and keys are sufficiently potent, a new electrical signal will be stimulated to move through the receiving neuron and repeat the process again ... and again ... and again ... for the lifetime of the body ... at a speed incomprehensible and invisible to our awareness.

The *space* appears to be the necessary third element in the transfer process. Without the space, the transfer of information could not happen. Information is encoded in the *frequency, quality,* and *pattern* of stimulating vibrations. If neurons were all directly connected, they would not be individuals. They would form one solid matrix. I wonder ... if the signal were uniform throughout ... without fluctuations in signal patterns ... then information encoded in these frequency patterns would be the same throughout the brain ... one, monotonous hum.

But with the synaptic space, the timing and content of molecular flow will vary slightly at each of millions, or billions, of synapses engaged at the moment. The pattern of those different times of release and renewed stimulation carries a code. Without the space to vary the timing of energy transfer, could any information be moved?

Yet, there is nothing in the space of its own. It is just the space between neurons. Inside the molecular world of these neurotransmitters is another dimension, the world of atoms. Inside the world of atoms, is a space which holds the world of sub-atomic "particles". Inside the world of particles, is the space between the tiniest particles. And ... given their infinitesimal size, these particles exist in a vast space of their own out of which they appear and disappear.

There is space inside of everything. The sperm must cross the space to the egg. An idea must travel the space between the point of its inception in my imagination and its influence out in the world. My feelings must cross the space between us so we may join in relationship. The relationship needs appropriate space to grow. "There is a crack, a crack in everything. That's how the light gets in."*

As Inside, So Outside: Everything out of Nothing

From the viewpoint of the space, both the infinitesimal world of quantum particles and the macro world of mass-based objects ... galaxies,

* *Leonard Cohen's, "Anthem"*

stars, planets, lifeforms, humans, you, and me ... are its offspring. From the quantum perspective, all the worlds, all the levels, both the large and small, are derived from and are part of and sustained by the underlying quantum realm.

It is the same space between atoms that allows them to move, reconfigure themselves, blend with other atoms to create new qualities with different properties. Inside each atom is vast space in which swim infinitesimal sub-atomic "particles", each spinning and vibrating in the same space of the quantum dimension. The formless, shapeless, "empty" space at this micro-micro-micro level of inner space is currently called, among other labels, the "Quantum Foam", the "space" from which subatomic particles appear and disappear.

Above our heads, beyond our atmosphere, the "ether" of philosophers, is now called by cosmologists the "void" or "vacuum" or *"outer space"* ... or ... *that-which-holds-the-eternal-infinite-vibrating-energy-of-the quantum-world* that has the potential to temporarily congeal into everything we call matter. Neurologists call this space *synapse*, the space between all the neurons in my brain. But ... everything, all forms and all information transfer ... all comes from/through the space between things. The space between the stars appears to be the same space as that between sub-atomic particles, inside the atoms, inside the molecules which combine to make the cells that combine to make and energize our bodies.

Following the ancient understanding of relationships phrased as "As Above, So Below", its corollary would be "As Inside, So Outside." What is our experience with the space, the synapse ...in a psychological sense? What is the equivalent of the inner space of our psychological world in relation to the space which holds the outside world?

Some neurologists and physicists have become brave enough to begin speculating that our physical brain is a structure which hosts the requirements for *quantum phenomena to produce the experience of consciousness*. From this perspective, our brains seem to be quantum computers. Subjective sensitivity, awareness, and varying degrees and qualities of consciousness appear related to the underlying vibratory dimension of sub-atomic particles ... or the void out of which they appear and disappear. If consciousness is a quality of the space, then consciousness also has contact with the macro universe without and the quantum psychological world within.

I now find my mind focused on holding onto my attention so as to con-

24

tinue to look simultaneously in both directions, inside my psychological world and outside to the physical world of clocks and trees, people, stars and events. I am trying to stay balanced between the two levels, outer material and inner psychological. I can feel the pull of each on my attention. My responsibility appears to be to bear this tension and maintain the balance. In the effort, I feel more energized.

As I look both ways ...out into the physical world around me and inward at the thoughts, impressions, feelings, reactions occurring in my psychological space... holding the two dimensions in relationship within me ... I seem to be experiencing this from the *space in between* ... the *Universal Synapse* between everything ... both *inside* and *outside* the moment, simultaneously. My awareness seems located in this Void. Am I experiencing what happens in my brain from the space between all my neurons? This viewpoint implies that consciousness is a property of the Synapse. It then follows that Consciousness is part of the fabric of the Universe. The part of *me* ... this composite creature made of matter: cells and molecules and atoms and sub-atomic particles ... that is mysteriously aware ... must then, also, be part of the fabric of the Cosmos.

How much of the All which can be experienced must depend on the type of brain each creature is designed to carry as a processing machine. In humans, with the most sophisticated processing apparatus currently known, the level and quality of our attention, our understanding, our values, and therefore, our level of consciousness, determines how much of the All our attention can notice and understand.

There are vast differences in capacity and motivation among people ... and within each given individual from moment to moment, mood to mood. At times this capacity can increase, as a result of training the brain through meditative traditions so that it becomes receptive to increasingly refined and enriched impressions ... or through psychoactive molecules in drugs ... near-death experiences ... or on rare occasions ... spontaneously and inexplicably.

Consciousness and Cosmos

Where is Consciousness to be found in relation to the Cosmological and the Sub-Atomic realms? Are not the outer and inner worlds, in a manner of speaking, united by Consciousness? Consciousness can be *conceptually* aware of both the higher and the lower, the enormous and the miniscule, simultaneously. Can we know that the Macro and the Micro exist when Consciousness is unaware of them? We assume they exist out of sight but, in the only sense that we can confirm, they exist in our awareness of them.

Regardless of that paradox, Consciousness is a phenomenon which can hold within itself the concept of both the large dimension of the Universe visible in *Outer* Space and the micro worlds of molecules, cells, atoms, and sub-atomic particles in the dimension of *Inner* Space.

Where then is the *Space of Consciousness*? It seems to be a Space where everything that exists can find a home. As Consciousness can hold in Mind an awareness and degree of understanding of them both, does this suggest that Consciousness is somehow 'larger' than the other dimensions combined or is intertwined with them?

The levels of the Universe contain things, whether solids, liquids, gases, or plasmas, on all scales. What is contained in the dimension of the *Space of Consciousness*?

Patterns of electrical energy flow through incalculable numbers of interconnecting neurons, currently estimated at 85 billion in the average brain. Our scientific instruments can now watch the movement of electrical currents and the patterns they form in relationship to what is being experienced in the brain. But instruments cannot "see" the content of a thought, a motivation or shift in a valuation. They cannot see what lies behind the visible manifestations in the invisible Space out of which emerge the patterns of our personality and our essence. We can *intuit* its reality in another person but it is invisible from the outside originating somewhere within the manifested form we can see, hear and touch. "Only by their fruits" can we know what is inside them. Yet, *we can see* our thoughts, motivations and shifts in valuation ... if we know how and where to look. Our *vantage point* appears to be *inside the Space which holds the thoughts, motivations,* and *values* we may, or may not, manifest outside our private awareness.

When we direct our attention into our own interior world, we discover it is not a vacuum but a world containing the forms of thoughts and memories, the feeling of emotions, the tactile experience of the body's memories. Much of what we may discover appears to be conditioned by interaction between events outside and our world inside - the biological survival mechanism and the conditioned reactions of our personality - thus creating a deeply patterned invisible architecture that we have mistaken for ourselves.

Where is this space? Is this another way of asking, what is the location of Mind? When I look inside at the field of my Awareness and am aware that *I* am looking, *I* don't seem to have any materiality. It certainly seems associated with my brain, but sometimes my experience of this quality in the moment feels much broader and extensive than just my head.

I have read a lot about the brain. As an assistant professor teaching a general psychology class, I once held one in my hand. I know from experience that I can time travel in my mind, that I have different levels of sensitivity. I know that I can "know" something but then "forget it" ... even forget that I once knew it ... until it 'pops' back into awareness.

We continue to discover unexpected structures and phenomena in the space between and within things. But regardless of how much more exists that we are yet to discover, the Space which holds it all remains untouched and unknown. This Space contains and interpenetrates everything, from material forms to potential pure energy. It lies between the galaxies and the stars, between the cells of our body and the atoms within those cells and the subatomic particles within those atoms. It holds our thoughts, our feelings, our memories, our understandings, our sense of ourselves and imaginations of others. It is the invisible realm from which all things that exist, from celestial bodies to atoms, to ourselves, originate at conception and return to at death.

Because it is invisible to our senses and our instruments, we rarely notice or think about it. For our ordinary consciousness, it does not exist. It is only empty space. Literally ... nothing. How can "nothing" have any importance? How can something come from nothing? How could one pay attention to "nothing"? We open to the world around us through our senses and are so filled with stimulation that we typically even forget to notice ourselves in the moment. If we turn our attention inside our body and mind, we typically discover a constant din of sensations, feeling, reactions, thoughts and fantasies such that we can find no quiet place free of subjective stimulation.

The Space of Neurotransmitters

In the introduction to this exploration, I referred to an impression I had experienced forty years earlier. Since that time, science has learned much about the activity occurring in the synapse and the role of neurotransmitters, specialized molecules that influence and direct the activity of the nervous system.

Wikipedia's definition: "A neurotransmitter is a *signaling* molecule secreted by a neuron or a glial cell to affect another cell across a synapse.

The cell receiving the signal, or target cell, may be another neuron, but could also be a gland or muscle cell."

Most of us have heard the names oxytocin, epinephrine, dopamine, serotonin, endorphins, amino acids. These molecules are prime regulators of our moods and behaviors. They are produced in the dendrites of a nerve cell body and are released to "float" across the synapse to the axon of the next cell body ... or multiple axons of other nerve cells, as many as a thousand other connecting nerve cells at each transmission. Each has a specialized shape that will only "fit" into an appropriately configured receptor on adjacent neuron axons. This "lock and key" model allows for extraordinary control of the complex information transfer required to operate a living organism. The questions of how they "float", what directs them, how they know where they are going, what determines how much and in what combinations the variety of neurotransmitters are dispatched to provide the desired stimulation at the right moment for the correct length of time, is ... unknown. The speed of these processes places them in a different "world" than ours ... neurotransmitters are said to influence their target cells within 1 to 500 milliseconds from release to docking, while the subsequent transmission along the neuron axon has been measured at speeds up to 270 meters per second.

The point I wish to make is that we now know that the "space" seems empty to our senses and requires increasingly sophisticated instruments to "see" down ... down ... deeper ... into the molecular-atomic-sub-atomic worlds. Yet, the newly discovered molecules live and move in a space. There does not seem to be a connecting structure guiding this activity ... and it is in the space *between* that a transfer of information is occurring in fragments to be reconstructed later. Recent photographs of cell bodies taken with new instrumentation, have disclosed previously undiscovered filaments, *microtubules*, inside the space of the cell which appear to connect and direct the activity of these molecules...as well as *transmit light*, the *biophotons* emitted by all living tissue. Once again, what initially looked like the final underlying "empty space" had been reached, new instruments show that even that apparently empty space still hosts energetic activity.

The Space of the Stars

When we look up into the night sky, we see pinpoints of light with vast black spaces in between. Until recently, this was also all that astronomers could see. The "materialized" objects in the Universe, stars, planets, gal-

Image 1. Pillars of Creation – a Stellar Nursery: NASA

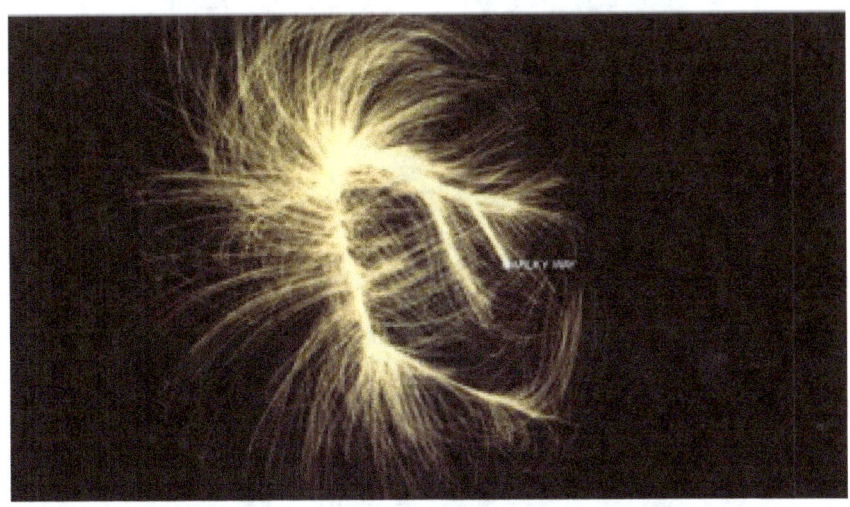

Image 2. Lanakea: Our Home Galactic Cluster NASA

As Inside, So Outside; As Above, So Below

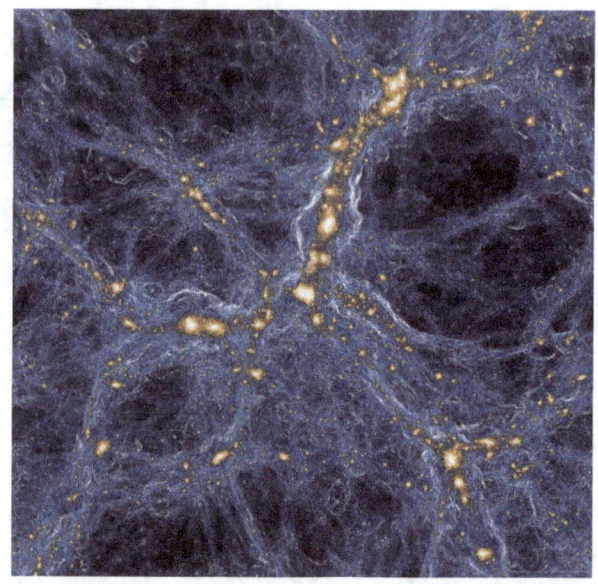

Image 3. Lanakea: Our Home Galactic Cluster (another view) NASA

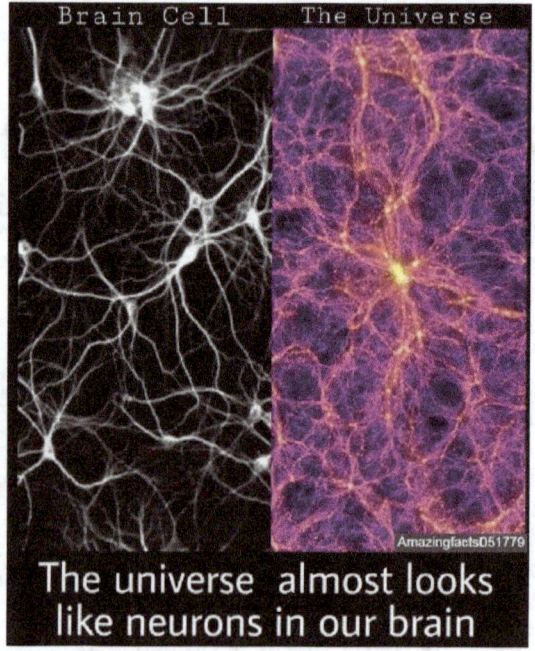

Image 4. Photos from Science and Technology's post

axies, nebulae, appear separated by unfathomable empty distances so large as to be measured in light years, the time that it would take light to travel at an estimated 186,000 Earth miles per second for 365 Earth days. We call this realm Outer *Space*.

Until recently, telescopic exploration could only record the light of stars and the reflection of our sun off planets, comets, asteroids. In the visible light spectrum, we could see nothing connecting these objects ... only what we call the "Void" or the "inky blackness of Outer Space". The current estimate is that materialized objects make up only 4% of the Universe. New NASA telescopes are increasingly designed to look at different spectrums other than visible light. What appears when we see into wavelengths that are not registered by *our senses* are amazing images of clouds and filaments and flashes of energy that connect and envelop the stars and galaxies. These clouds are partially composed of organic molecules that are the basis for life.

Astronomers believe that these clouds serve as stellar nurseries, structures in themselves which have a purpose and function ...a celestial 'womb' to 'birth and nourish' stars. Or ... it may be that the stars have a purpose and function and are there to take care of the filaments .... or it may be that both together have an additional function and purpose beyond our current understanding to something else yet to be discovered. With new instruments we can now see the shape of these connecting, harboring "bodies", but we cannot "see" the origin of their purpose or function. That lies in the space which contains and interpenetrates them.*

Large clusters of galaxies are now recognized to also be linked together by filament structures, a universal architecture invisible to us until recently which form a pattern of networks that looks very much like pictures of neuronal networks in a brain. The galaxies are carried along invisible "rivers" of connections. Our Supercluster, named in Hawaiian, "Lanakea", meaning *Immense Heaven*, is a community of an estimated 100,000 galaxies, all flowing, or being pulled, towards something invisible, named "The Great Attractor" believed to be another much larger cluster.†

Comparisons of organic structures at the cellular level look very much like the unexpected images we are now receiving from the formerly presumed "empty" spaces between the stars and galaxies. The ancient adage "As Above So Below" captures the similarity in forms between the

* See Image 1, page 29
† See Images 2 page 29 and 3, page 30, opposite

cosmological and biological shapes. In biology, it is understood that form follows function. If this is applied to the celestial levels, the forms now coming into view suggest that when we look up, we are looking into a living organism which we, and everything we see, are a part of.

There are new theories in physics that suggest that the "vacuum" of outer space is not an empty void but is full of energy down to the "Planck" level (the hypothesized smallest possible unit of anything) where we have discovered endless vibrations underlying the smallest units of energy in the quantum realm. From *where* is the foundational impulse to maintain this vibration originating? It must be in the Space beyond, between and within the vibrating energy units.

Conclusion

We have looked at the biological and cosmological relationships...and we have explored a third Cosmos which, in a sense, encompasses and/or interpenetrates the other two. The dimension of Consciousness has an enormous range of qualities, from the sensitivity of a flat worm to the insight of a human sage. And, human beings demonstrate a range of levels of consciousness and sensitive awareness both within each individual over time as well as between all the individuals in a population.

From the viewpoint of the quantum vacuum, both the infinitesimal world of quantum particles and the macro world of mass-based objects built on the foundation of quantum particles ... including lifeforms ... are its offspring. From the perspective of the quantum realm, both the large and small worlds are parts, extensions, and expressions, of ... itself!

If Consciousness is a quality of the subatomic level, then Consciousness also has contact with the macro universe without and the quantum world within.

Where then is the location of Mind? If Mind is a phenomenon embedded within the *space* encompassing the quantum level of sub-atomic activity, then Mind would be Universal and at the root of Existence. And *my mind* would be an infinitesimal aspect of the underlying quantum world. If I am Mind, then my home must also be in the collective activity of the Void out of which all existence has emerged and to which it returns. The span of my Attention circumscribes the scope and depth of my Mind in that moment.

Where Mind is, there is Attention ...and where Mind's Attention is, there I Am.

Addendum

Current discoveries suggest intriguing similarities between the 'laws" of the quantum world compared with our observations of the subjective world of conscious experience.

1. Non-Determinism:

Quantum Mechanics: Quantum systems are inherently probabilistic, with particles often described as existing in superpositions of states until measured.

Psychological Functioning: While psychological processes are influenced by many factors, human behavior is also probabilistic, shaped by a combination of genetic, environmental, and individual factors.

2. Observer Effect:

Quantum Mechanics: The act of measurement in quantum mechanics can influence the state of particles, known as the observer effect.

Psychological Functioning: In psychology, the presence of an observer or researcher can influence how individuals behave or respond, known as the Hawthorne effect.

3. Uncertainty:

Quantum Mechanics: Heisenberg's Uncertainty Principle states that you cannot simultaneously know a particle's position and momentum with absolute certainty.

Psychological Functioning: The human mind often operates with inherent uncertainty, as thoughts, emotions, and behaviors are not always predictable or fully understood.

4. Interconnectedness:

Quantum Mechanics: Quantum entanglement suggests that particles can be interconnected, and the state of one particle can affect the state of another, even at a distance.

Psychological Functioning: Human experiences and relationships are interconnected, where one's emotional state or actions can impact others' well-being and behavior.

5. Emergent Properties:

Quantum Mechanics: Quantum systems can exhibit emergent properties that are not easily predictable from the properties of individual particles.

Psychological Functioning: Complex psychological phenomena, like consciousness or intelligence, can emerge from the interactions of simpler cognitive and neural processes.

The Lattice

My friend and mentor, Dr. Keith Buzzell, said to me once that ideas are the building blocks of concepts and theories. When they are stacked and tied to each other in a particular pattern, they form a lattice in the conceptual part of my mind. However, as exciting as ideas may be to my mind, of themselves they are of no practical use unless put into action in some way. Yet it is at the point of initiating into the material level of reality from the germ of a thought that the results become uncertain, often misguided, impractical or just outright wrong and damaging.

A lattice is a skeleton, an outline of a potential, a form waiting to be filled, to support what it is constructed to hold. Filled with what? Supporting what? Filled with actual experience! Without a lattice to arrange themselves within, experiences would have no way to be organized, understood and acted upon in a consistent way. There would be no conceptual framework to support them. Without a mental framework, how could consciousness read their patterns or learn from them? But without experience, the lattice is only theory ... an intellectual skeleton in the mind holding nothing but potential.

Theories not based on actual experience and replication rarely prove valid. Science is a system of search that first observes, then theorizes about what it observes, then tests to see if the same observations predicted by the theory can be consistently replicated, especially by others, without the risk of bias that the creator of the theory carries. In our individual, non-scientifically led lives, we rarely use this type of process to confirm our theories and opinions.

On the other hand, experiences not organized in a framework, cannot be understood as part of a larger whole. They are likely to be seen as singular events when they might also be seen as part of a pattern. The only one who can make this determination is the one who is having the experience. If an idea cannot eventually be linked with experience, then any initiative comes only from unsubstantiated theory. ... a manifestation of imagination.

Experiences are the materials of life from which theories are born and, simultaneously, the laboratory where theories can be tested for their utility and explanatory power. If a plan of action comes only from the shape of an empty lattice devoid of confirming experience, assume that the initiative will be premature, naïve or ignorant and the results likely to be disappointing.

Why don't we recognize and accept this? Three reasons come to mind.

First, occasionally, we get lucky and the theory was useful enough to bring the result hoped for. This intermittent reinforcement strengthens a habit and is the conditioned pattern most resistant to change.

Second, typically, when our theory is not confirmed, we tend to blame something or someone else rather than ourselves.

Third, we tend to attach our theories and opinions to our sense of self, self-respect, self-worth. When I identify myself with my thinking, a criticism of the theory or idea is experienced as an attack on me, personally. If I change my mind, even based on new experience, I might feel or look weak, an admission that I was wrong. Then the lattice becomes my shield and I ignore the non-confirming experiences flowing through it.

A *frame-of-mind* is a lattice built of blocks of ideas and attitudes ... a perpetual lens of specific shape and orientation that, because of its structure, will be biased to see somethings and to be blind to others. The space between the framework channels the flow of experiences ... feeling, sensation, learning. Has the lattice, as a pre-existing theory, shaped perception of the pattern of the experiences into a self-fulfilling prophecy... or ... has the framework grown out of actual observation of the continuous flow of life, thus having its roots in experience?

A house cannot be constructed without a plan, a skeleton to support what will eventually fill it. One cannot live in the frame alone. The walls must be filled with rooms, furniture, utilities ... and people ... otherwise there is no point to the house. But a house of rooms, furniture, utilities, and people cannot exist without a framework to hold it.

Perhaps we could metaphorically say that the lattice is like light when light behaves like a particle. It is a more solid something. Experience, on the other hand, is spontaneous, fluid, unpredictable. It is more like light when it behaves like a wave. What ties the two together is the processing power, the organizing capacities of the mind that is having the experience and looking for a framework in which to categorize the experience and see how it links with other events in life … the life without and the life within.

As Inside, So Outside; As Above, So Below

Quotations

It is first of all necessary to make the organ of vision analogous and similar to the object to be contemplated. Never would the eye have perceived the sun if it had not first taken the form of the sun; likewise, the soul cannot see beauty unless it first becomes beautiful itself, and every man must make himself beautiful and divine in order to attain the sight of beauty and divinity.

Plotinus

A human being is part of a whole, called by us Universe. A part limited in time and space, he experiences himself, his thoughts, and feelings as something separated from the rest ... a kind of optical delusion of his consciousness. The striving to free oneself from the confines of the ego, that moment of ecstasy, that experience of Eternity, right here is the one issue of true religion.

Einstein

All Truth passes through three stages. First it is ridiculed. Second, it is violently opposed. Third, it is accepted as being self-evident.

Arthur Schopenhauer

As Inside, So Outside; As Above, So Below

The Divine State of Confusion

Confusion is generally understood as an intellectual/emotional state characterized by lack of clarity, uncertainty, and doubt, which then typically manifests as indecision and hesitation or rejection. We often experience this condition of lack as uncomfortable, potentially dangerous, and/or a sign of weakness. Depending on how one interprets the situation about which one is confused, the degree of emotional distress resulting from the felt pressure to "know" for certain can lead to anxiety, depression, impulsiveness or paralysis and other indications of mental/emotional distress.

This can arise from different sources. I may lack the necessary information required to make a quality choice on an issue. For example, I was expecting you to call at 5 pm. It is now 7 pm. What has happened? Have you forgotten? Are you injured? Did I misunderstand our agreement? Did you? Do I have the date wrong? Do you? Has your phone stopped working? Should I be worried, hurt, insulted, angry? This is very atypical of you. Without knowing the reason that you did not call, I don't know how to feel or act. I am confused.

A different situation arises when my belief system is challenged. What do I do with the discordant information? Do I ignore or reject it? What if it is correct? Does that mean my beliefs, perhaps my values, are based on an incomplete or false understanding of the situation?

For example, early in my studies of Gurdjieff's ideas, I had been very intrigued. Then I came across an idea that made no sense to me. The first reaction from my intellect was that the proposition seemed grossly unscientific, superstitious, logically outrageous. I felt I had hit a stone wall and could go no further. Then, a second internal voice began to talk softly to me. "Had I found the ideas up to this point of use?" "Yes. Absolutely". I was stunned by their ability to suggest a model for phenomena whose existence never seemed answerable by current scientific understanding. This second voice suggested that since, up until that moment, I had found the ideas of great value, that perhaps my negative reaction to this one was because I *might not understand* what was being said. I could not assess whether it was a metaphor or meant literally. "Perhaps", the voice suggested, I should "just put this idea on a mental shelf and continue reading".

Fortunately, I did so. As time passed, other inexplicable ideas joined it on my waiting list. What also happened is that from time to time, I would have a new impression of my inner processes and one of the sequestered ideas would jump off the shelf into my lap in association with the new experience. In such moments, I would realize that *this experience* was what *that* strange idea was referring to. I had not initially understood it because I lacked the resonant experience which it was describing. I learned to sit patiently with my confusion until clarity appeared at a later time.

A helpful way I found for dealing with states of confusion was to deconstruct the word confusion.

A standard dictionary definition of 'fusion" is: "an act of fusing or melting together, or union, joining or co-mingling." But as a prefix, "con" is an abbreviation for "contra" meaning "against" as in opposition or disagreement or in debating the pros and cons of an issue.

A situation producing *con*fusion, represents a challenge to what had previously been "fused" as an understanding of reality, a believed "fact" based on a melding of experiences and learnings that had been accepted as truth. When sufficiently challenged, my belief in that "fact" is broken apart. Its "fusion" no longer holds. The new information or experience has fractured the firmly held structure of thought or belief. What had once felt certain can no longer hold together. The new perspective dissolves my mental/emotional status quo and puts me into the state of confusion. I suddenly feel "the ground shift under me", "I can't get my footing", "I don't know where things stand", "I feel lost". "I am un-moored".

Nothing can change without undergoing a transition phase. When that transition occurs in my mind, previously held understanding, opinions, and beliefs, must first come apart to allow for the formation of a new mental or attitudinal reconfiguration. Depending on my tolerance for this type of disruption in my psychological world, my response may range from excitement at one end to hostility or fear at the other.

Were this not possible, my mind and feelings would be frozen in their previously acquired form. I could learn nothing new. Ironically, whatever belief or interpretation I stand on to reject the new implications of the discordant information or experience, may, itself, once have disrupted a previously held belief.

Going back to my experience with the ideas of G.I. Gurdjieff, I find that what happened to me corresponds exactly to what is formulated as a "paradigm shift", an alteration in an established way of understanding. As living organisms fight to survive, so do belief systems. Paradigms, whether of a scientific, philosophical, political, religious, or personal nature, are loath to permit discrepant information or impressions to penetrate and disturb them. To the degree which time, effort, and utility support the current "fusion" of information and its underlying beliefs and attitudes, new information should be required to reach a high bar in order to produce a shift, a *de*-fusion of the current status quo. A melding of one's self-image or self-esteem with current beliefs: political, religious, or scientific, can, however, result in an inflexible rigidity that rejects perspectives that may carry more accurate or more potent understanding. Under this circumstance, a change of mind would threaten my sense of self and will be strongly resisted.

The psychological state of confusion is a *transition zone*, an experience of the fabric of the old dissolving and not yet replaced with the new. It is a necessary stage of transformation from one viewpoint to a different viewpoint. Without this transition, nothing new can appear. If the pupa could think and feel, would it be in a state of confusion inside its chrysalis prior to emerging as a butterfly... if not in its cocoon, then certainly on emerging as something entirely different than what it had known itself to be? Confusion is a frequent characteristic of stages of human development and learning. Unexpected changes of fortune which upset pre-established patterns of living and understanding, often produce a period of confusion until a new stability of circumstance and perspective can be developed. "How could this be happening? I don't believe it! I reject this!"

A synonym for confused is "bewildered" ... to find oneself in a "wilderness", a place unknown, a place never before visited ... at least by oneself. There is no map. The only solution is to accept the reality of the new situation, take a deep breath and, with an open mind, begin to explore the new terrain. Only by accepting and exploring can we build a new map of our situation and possibilities. If one accepts, rather than fights, the state of confusion, there will eventually appear a new understanding and a new direction. The new experiences will eventually blend, fuse into something different than what preceded it.

I call the State of Confusion, "Divine." What is the meaning of Divine? Typical usage historically has religious references, godlike, angelic, seraphic, saintly, beatific, spiritual, heavenly, celestial, holy, relating to or coming from God or a god *divine*, will/law/love/inspiration.

In our modern, scientific, rational age, we do not ascribe the cause of phenomena to these older poetic ideas. Nevertheless, even when citing theories of the fundamental laws of the Universe in scientific language, creation remains a mystery. Knowing how something happens does not necessarily address the *meaning* of its happening ... whether the creation of the Universe, the creation of Life or the creation of a book or painting, or a sudden insight or inspiration or a "change of mind", a "shift of attitude", an alteration in understanding. Initially, there is the status quo. Then, suddenly, something has changed. The old is confronted with something outside of its paradigm. The former fusion of beliefs has begun to come apart. A new state appears.

This is a state in which the old no longer is unchallenged but perhaps something new has not yet become clear. Or, perhaps, a new viewpoint has suddenly, unexpectedly, appeared but will take a period of time to be digested and be accepted. The new situation or conclusion may not be to our liking. It may in fact be very challenging, but it has a level of reality that must be addressed.

"How has this happened?" "This cannot be!". "I have no idea what to do." "I've never been in a situation like this before". I don't know the rules". Such moments are an opening to a new creation: a new concept, a new perspective, a new opportunity, a new challenge, the dissolving of one set of assumptions and the expanding of beliefs to include previously unincluded possibilities ... whether for good or for ill.

Whether my confusion concerns phenomena of my personal life, such as how to solve a problem, or unexpected disruptions in relationships, or my tendency to make the same mistakes repeatedly ... or why human life seems so conflictual and chaotic ... the confusion is a manifestation that I am lacking information or perspective or sufficient experience to put the puzzle pieces together in a new way. It is an opportunity to expand myself.

The appearance of the Universe, the existence of Life, the reality of my being a *Consciousness* inside an animal body, are all manifestations of a mysterious creative impulse beyond our conceptual understanding. We live with the confusion of this reality without an answer. We tend to deal with this state of perplexity by either ignoring it ... or accepting on faith a theological version of the mystery given by a religion ... or the mechanistic viewpoint of modern science.

Or, we may spend a lifetime in pursuit of a satisfactory way of comprehending through a direct experiencing of the mystery. The former are defenses against confusion. The latter is an acceptance of the invitation to bear not knowing ... while *simultaneously* feeling the longing to understand.

To accept to be in a state of confusion, whether about either ordinary or existential questions, is an acceptance of an invitation to a relationship with what is calling from beyond my present paradigm. It is an invitation to open my heart and mind to another perspective. It is a doorway to the dimension of other possibilities not yet known. In this sense it is a creative act. Our current understanding of the Creation, its meaning beyond even its mechanics, remains a mystery out of reach. The possibility of change, surprise, growth, is what allowed for the appearance of the Universe, the appearance of Life and the conception of me within the body of my mother from the fusion of sperm and ovum. Any new fusion is inevitably followed by coming apart and re-blending, the coming apart of the new blending and the reconfiguration with something else.

This is the process of Creation. For something new to appear, there must be three factors: the current understanding or paradigm ... the challenge of a different possibility of a compelling nature ... and the space, the openness, the environment, the willingness to allow the confusion of a confrontation of the old and the new... without rushing ... that allows time for the two to fuse into something new.

We can "explain" this mysterious creative impulse as an aspect of the "Laws of Nature", but that is only a relabeling of what has been more poetically understood to be a *creative process* originating from a higher level than ordinary life. It has been called the "realm of the gods" if one is a Pantheist or the realm of God if one is a monotheist. A 14th century usage as a verb meant "to discover by intuition or insight ... itself a process of continuing mystery and source of confusion for those attempting to explain it in neurological terms. The Proto-Indo-European root meaning is: to shine, with subsequent derivations such as sky, heaven, god.

After the State of Confusion dissolves, the new understanding shines a different light. In this sense, our ability to experience the State of Confusion is a gift of the divine mystery underlying the Universe.

Knowledge

G urdjieff said knowledge is "material" ... that everything is material ... "even God". For years I could make no sense of this assertion until I turned to science. My conclusions may not be what he had in mind, but they give me a base to work from.

Yesterday I read a review of a recently published book concerning the effervescent nature of Knowledge and the question of why libraries have so often been deliberately destroyed in warfare and books burned by religious and ideological fanatics. Why is knowledge such a threat that one's enemy would deliberately target your knowledge base ... as if knowledge did not belong to them as well? Aside from the always present threat of barbarism to the thrust of civilized evolution, the question caused me to think about the mysterious nature of what we call Knowledge.

Science tells us that Matter, materiality, is a densified state of Energy ... and Energy is de-densified Matter ... This is the point of $E = mc^2$. The amount of energy is equivalent to the amount of mass times a constant, the speed of light ... 186,000 miles per second ... *squared*! The tiniest particle of matter contains unimaginable potential energy binding it together. The atomic bomb erupts from the splitting of atoms of a heavy element like uranium or plutonium. The energy that bound the atoms together is released and appears on the Earth as a representative of the Sun.

All energy is potential matter, and all matter is potential energy ... the yin and yang.

So ... how can we think about Knowledge as material? Knowledge could be thought of as potential energy that takes the form of thoughts, images, symbols, when the vibration of that energy reverberates in a mind. Whatever realization appears in that mind can then be transferred to another mind through the appropriate stimulation, by vibration, of sensory organs and subsequent electrical impulses which race into the next brain to re-create, in that other mind, a facsimile of what is being transmitted.

The transference from one mind to the next is initiated by another transformation of the data into a manifestation of energy as movement, sound, facial or body gesture, writing, painting and other expressions that carry the essence of information to be transmitted back into symbolic form ready for the next receiver.

The information itself is not the wave of photonic energy that brings images to our eyes or air pressure that vibrates our eardrums and stimulates the electrical response in our bodies ... it is a pattern of vibration in the energetic impulses that symbolically carries qualities of the source which it represents as an emissary from the dimension of its essence. It is as if the source has expanded itself by implanting vibrations of its essence within whatever energy emanates from it. In fact, we might say that *radiating and emanating energy represents the essence of the identity of the source*. It is like a fingerprint of the source, a holographic extension. Each is unique. That essence is the potential content that can be noticed and decoded by a mind.

For example, starlight is composed of wavelengths of the elements which constitute the star. Received on Earth, that light will display different wave bands, each indicating the elemental and chemical composition of the light source. Since the light expanding from the source carries the imprint of that source, in a way, we have direct access even over billions of light-years. Astronomers who study exo-planets as they pass in front of their home stars, and thus "read" the chemical composition of their atmosphere, have already discovered the basic organic chemistry needed for life on worlds in other solar systems.

Closer to home, light bouncing off the face of my friend will display muscular changes in expression. Sound waves from my friend's vocal cords will bring to my ears tonal qualities that give me an understanding of my friend's emotional state as they reflect the mood and affect in that moment of my friend's psychological world.

The degree of potential decodable energy depends on the type, quality and training of the mind it enters. The mind of a snail, the mind of a dog, the mind of a human, are each a receiving apparatus of different capacities. Whatever they are programed to be receptive to, whether only a heat differential or the smell of a buried bone, or an insight into the mystery of creation, that decipherable range of vibration becomes the information which shapes the world in which the receiver perceives its existence.

We call this "information" ... in-form ... to acquaint, apprise, notify, to make one aware of something. Inform implies the imparting of knowledge, especially of facts or occurrences from the Latin root, *informare*, "train or instruct," and literally "shape or form." Intuitively, we understand that the vibrations of many wavelengths impinging on our senses acquaint, inform and shape what we experience and assume is the only reality that can exist. The vibration takes *form* in a mind.

From our ordinary perspective, there seems to be nothing there. From the level of our senses, nothing 'solid' has been transferred. At a different level, a level only we can see, inside ourselves, there is a noticing of the appearance of a change in understanding in our minds from the implantation of the coded vibrations. In another sense, when Knowledge "materializes" inside the receiver, what is being transmitted has potential power to produce changes in thinking, feeling, perception and ultimately in behavior. It carries a potential motivating power ... again, depending on the receptivity of the recipient.

It is in this sense, that I can think of Knowledge as a form of matter ... albeit too rarified to be visible to my external senses. It can be transferred. It can be discovered. It can be lost. It can be shared or withheld. It can be carried, hidden and stored. It can be divided and doled out in parts. It can be refreshed and altered. Its value and potency vary depending on its content, the relevance of that content to the situation to which it is applied and the understanding of that content by the receiver. Knowledge has to be kept safe from deterioration, or distortion, or destruction or decay. Perhaps some knowledge is too dangerous, too harmful to reveal because it would be misunderstood or deliberately misused depending on the level of understanding and quality of Being of the receiver of that Knowledge. Because Knowledge can only be transferred from mind to mind, some Knowledge cannot be given out too widely or indiscriminately. It may require help to be assimilated. It must be sufficiently focused and concentrated to be transmitted in its entirety. It may be of such complexity that it must be disseminated in a specific sequence over time in order to be appropriately absorbed. Depending on its content, it may need the receiving mind to be prepared for its reception ahead of time. If spread too thin, it may have little impact or even a negative influence when insufficiently understood.

This must be why Knowledge is so dangerous to totalitarian individuals and governments. Knowledge is a form of energy that changes minds. Changed minds change perspectives. Changed perspectives lead to changed behaviors. Changed behaviors will disturb the status quo. Knowledge can transform a person. What is put into a mind determines the manifestations of the person. Control the mind, control the person. Do I ever wonder who controls my mind?

But this is only the mechanical aspect. Let us stipulate that Knowledge is some form of energy that has been alchemically organized into a mental-emotional-sensory format such that the meaning is embedded in the architecture of the words or images or movements that carry the energy from one mind to another, from one heart to another, from one body to another.

Where is Knowledge stored? In materialized form, historically, it has been encoded symbolically into books, pictures, dance, story ... and internally, symbolically encoded into patterns of neuronal connections which then present to our mind what we call memory ... words, pictures, stories we see and hear and feel in our head, in our feelings and our body, so as to re-live the event as remembered. The advent of computers allows for knowledge transfer in 1's and 0's. Quantum computers transfer knowledge through the manipulations of sub-atomic particles. But the information is still encoded in the pattern.

Knowledge is also stored in the minds and experiences of those who possess it ... and in the artifacts which they produce to symbolically represent the Knowledge encoded in their minds.

As an organized pattern of energy in the mind, Knowledge also can be thought of as having a quality of materiality since it can be "weighed" and valued, its application can be narrow or broad, it can affect little or much, it may be emotional, physical, intellectual or a blending. We can have weighty thoughts or light ones, consequential or superfluous.

Where and how is Knowledge acquired in the first place? Someone had to make a discovery ... a dis-cover ... an un-covering of something that was waiting to be noticed. A mind notices something that interests it. The energy of *attention* inherent within it, flows towards that which captured its interest. Typically, the attention is "captured" and "held" until the "interest" weakens. Until that point, as attention watches, new patterns are discerned. New connections between things appear in the watching mind. A change in the state of understanding occurs. A new "knowing" appears in the mind.

But where was that Knowledge prior to a mind noticing its footprint in the pattern? It obviously is imbedded in the fabric of what attention focused upon. Attention *extracts* it from the background.

As scientists discover more and more about the nature of the Universe, they are looking into the Cosmos to discover patterns that can translate into Knowledge in the mind of the scientist ... who can then share it with other "like-minds". As meditators discover more and more about the nature of themselves, they are looking into their own minds and feelings to discover the patterns that will transform into Knowledge about themselves. Gurdjieff advised that to learn about Man, one should study the Universe and to learn about the Universe, one needs to study Oneself ... as the Universe is in us and we are in the Universe. As above, so below. As inside, so outside.

How to share this new perspective with the minds of others which have not yet made this discovery? How to assist in the re-ordering of energy patterns in their minds so that they can themselves experience the discovery of the new perspective as it now begins to appear to them inside their own mind? Modeling, demonstrating, explaining in words, gestures, may ignite a resonant light of recognition in the next mind. In this way, knowledge is spread like bacteria and like bacteria, some knowledge is beneficial and some is deleterious. Whatever the content of this knowing, in order to be kept alive, it must become a transmission from generation to generation like an oral tradition.

When the guardians of the Knowledge die, where does the Knowledge they carried go?

A few examples of very ancient knowledge have survived until today in the form of myth and epic poetry, passed on through the conservatorship of still living bards, or shards of broken pottery, or paintings on cave walls. Some was encoded in scrolls or totems or music or dance. Perhaps, someone who overheard something, now carries a fragment of the Knowledge. Perhaps there are other fragments of the original whole being carried by other minds. Over generations, these fragments may meet and merge, sometimes amplifying each other, sometimes degrading each other. Perhaps, sometime in the future these different strands once again find each other in the mind of a startled person whose sudden insight lights up their inner world. Now the Knowledge is their responsibility to keep alive and pass on before their death.

It is said that Knowledge is power ... and what is power, but energy? Mortal enemies intuitively sense this. To destroy the Knowledge base of your opponent destroys their power and makes turning them into a subject population much easier. How much Knowledge, once discovered, disseminated, and utilized, has been lost, perhaps forever? When the Spanish conquerors burned the literature of the native Indian cultures, the history of a civilization and a continent was lost. How many generations, or millennia, must pass before Knowledge lost is rediscovered … if ever?

But, for the wise who value it for its own sake, Knowledge may be seen as a portal, a connection to the dimension of pure potential energy that appears to underlie Existence … but not all knowledge is of the same quality. The knowledge of who said what to who about whom, the knowledge of farming potatoes, the knowledge of grooming horses, the knowledge of the forces of the universe, the knowledge of the lives of the Saints, the knowledge of good and evil … are all of different qualities, potentialities and value. In this way there can be high knowledge and low knowledge, practical knowledge and philosophical knowledge, scientific knowledge, and spiritual knowledge. How these different qualities are discerned and utilized depends on the level of Being of the user … hence the uneven results throughout history from the application of knowledge.

All brains are designed to search for patterns that facilitate survival of the organism. Mammals and birds transfer their knowledge base, both that of the species programmed instincts, but also individually acquired and transferred through modeling and demonstration. The human also uses these methods but adds to them the transfer of information through symbolism, words, diagrams, books and today through electronic storage and quantum energy transfer. The human ability to make discoveries in the invisible realm of conceptualizations, brings a capacity to acquire, store and utilize knowledge to re-direct energy and alter matter.

Our capacity to discover, process, store, and transfer knowledge, across space and time, is both curse and gift. Ageless folk-wisdom declares that "a little knowledge is a dangerous thing". Its misapplication can damage and destroy worlds. Its appropriate use is a gift from the gods, an invitation to come closer to them and discover the divine creative nature hidden within each of us. Knowledge appears, lives, and exercises its power from the invisible dimension of Mind … itself, a combination of bio-chemical, electrical and quantum phenomena. Understanding is experience-based and can be discovered and transferred like knowledge.

Although seemingly immaterial from the limitations of our bodily senses, the power to create and move worlds inherent in Knowledge clearly interacts with and shapes the world of materiality. Matter is created from energy, directed by energy, moved by energy, and ultimately transformed back into energy. What can grasp both ends of this pole, is the Mind and Knowledge imbues the mind with a power that can create or destroy. Knowledge is not only a materialized understanding, but the entry into material life of a power from a higher dimension.

As Inside, So Outside; As Above, So Below

Spiritual Transformation and Psychotherapy

This conversation is for people who sense a profound mystery behind the reality of life, behind the reality of themselves ... a mystery that neither science nor religion has adequately addressed for them. How to search for this mystery? How to verify this deeper reality through direct experience rather than theory or theology?

My experience, as a psychologically trained and oriented person, has convinced me that this mystery, this missing link between science and religion, science and what we call "spirit"*, is *Consciousness*† itself. Without the capacity for Awareness, there would be no mind to witness, theorize, investigate, and pursue answers to its questions. Without Awareness there are no questions.

What is this Awareness? Does it have different qualities, different levels, different intensities and dimensions? Can one grow or develop increased sensitivity to this finer, higher quality? What is the way, the method?

What are the implications of this *fact* ... this fact that *Awareness* is the *container* and the *digester* of what it encompasses? All that 'exists' for that Awareness, in any given moment, is what lies within the sphere of its attention ... and the field of that attention continually fluctuates on both a vertical and horizontal dimension from lower to higher levels, broader or more narrow, deeper or more shallow perspectives, from moment to moment throughout life.

How to explore this question in a way that isn't only technical or philo-sophical in language, but also, at times, perhaps poetic ... and also practical?

I also have wished to heal, at least for myself, the tension between sci-

---

* Spirit: *"the non-physical part of a person that is the seat of emotions and character; the soul ... in a human being thought to give the body life, energy, and power"*
† Consciousness:. *"the state of being aware of one's own existence, sensations, thoughts, surrounding"*, (Oxford Languages)

ence and religion... or the realm of higher, finer, subjective experience. Religion tells us, there are higher levels of reality, higher levels of emotionality, higher levels of discernment and understanding, that can be experienced inside of oneself. It states as a fact that, "the Kingdom lies within".

Science is now revealing to us a similar perspective ... that everything we can observe, study, and understand ... everything we experience as "reality" ... appears to us *inside* our brain and nervous system. We observe the outer world of material bodies and the forces that appear to govern them from *inside our subjective psychological world*, inside our brains. In that sense, the world that appears to be outside our bodies is, actually, a *simulation in our brains of what lies outside*. The subjective experience of everything lies "within."

Our senses are calibrated to pick up signals within different electromagnetic wavebands. Phenomena radiating above or below that narrow band of human sensitivity are not perceptible to us. Historically, this has understandably led many to assume that if it can't be seen and measured, it does not exist. The invention of instruments to extend our senses, such as telescopes, microscopes, electron colliders, PET scans, X-rays, infrared night goggles, allows an augmentation of our senses permitting us to peer into dimensions of reality previously inaccessible to our minds through sense organs alone.

Both approaches ... studying the outer world and studying our inner subjective world ... occur inside the sphere of our awareness. This holds the key and the greatest mystery .... a mystery, perhaps, greater than the origins of the materialized Universe. How does Awareness appear in the Universe, ... an Awareness that seems to be a quality of the mysterious force or energy we call life?

Humankind's Blindspot

Our awareness is typically focused on the reactions within, or between, our three functional centers ... instinct/sensation, emotion, and intellect ... and their interpretation and perception of the meaning of what is entering through the senses from the outside world. However, these three centers of functionality are heavily *programed* by everyday interaction with the life around us to assume that one's *interpretation of the meaning* of one's perceptions accurately represents total reality from the outside.

These responses are experienced in our fluctuating sphere of

Awareness ...and attention is then *consumed* by the experience. It loses contact with the reality of itself as the *Experiencer* of what the attention brings into Awareness. We only experience the programed response of our organism and believe that is all there is to reality. What is required is becoming aware of myself as the *possessor of the Awareness ... or the Awareness itself ... inside a biological machine* from within which I *notice* reactions occurring in my body and personality as responses to either inner or outer stimuli.

The Spiritual Marketplace

Throughout history, this search has been guided by shamans, seers, initiated elders and eventually priests, monks and others. In our contemporary secularized society, many have now substituted science and psychotherapy for philosophy and religion while others seek out meditation retreats and organized programs designed to use a mixture of techniques to facilitate emotional and insightful experiences. Others still explore the traditional religious paths through ashram or monastery. The current recognition from modern medicine of the medicinal possibilities for healing from the use of psychedelic plants to produce mind altering experiences, has revived popular interest in our species' first tool for exploring the inner dimensions.

The exploding Western spiritual marketplace today seems to be a manifestation of a shift in the communal society away from traditional religions of the past two and a half millennia and towards a different way of inner search. I believe that this heralds a direction of the new religions of the next millennium, a direction into oneself. ... the remaining unexplored frontier.

But what will be sought, found, and settled for? How deep does my interior go? How deep do I want to go ... am I prepared to go? And for what reason? This approach is a razor's edge. Unless one's egoism and distortions in self-image and self-understanding are sufficiently diminished and understood, the journey into self can turn narcissistic. The journey into oneself is not the same journey as into the *Self.*

This quest occurs in the *emotional* and *conceptual* realms which are inaccessible, and of little interest, to modern current hard science, which focuses its prodigious strengths on understanding how the mass-based world operates. To explore the realm of the Psyche requires a different mode of instrumentation than the study of the world outside.

The question then becomes, what is my motivation for such a deep dive into my mind and how deep do I wish to go? Is there something in me I wish to escape? Is there a sense of something missing I wish to find?

Quality and Levels

Everything that exists is organized in hierarchies ... by size, age, function, power, frequency, intensity ... and quality. In ordinary life we recognize degrees of initiation, expertise, training, sophistication. In any area of study or competence one begins as a novice. After long apprenticeship one becomes a competent technician, then craftsman. A few go deeper and become masters of the craft ... and the teachers of the craftsmen who then becomes teachers of the novices.

The same inescapable parameters are involved in spiritual pursuits. In traditions and "schools", there is a form, sequence and methodology underlying the bringing of a spiritual novice to deeper levels within themselves over time. In the language of the great religious traditions, these three levels of understanding and capacity are called *exoteric*, *mesoteric* and *esoteric*. My experience tells me that both public contemporary religious expressions as well as modern psychotherapy, for the most part, represent understanding of the psyche at the first two tiers. With the exception, perhaps, of the depth psychologies wielded by therapists of profound wisdom, the esoteric level has remained deep within ancient monasteries, ashrams, and secret "mystery schools" ... the esoteric core of all religions ... and accessible only through long mentorship.

Three Levels of Understanding: Exoteric, Mesoteric, Esoteric.

When someone realizes what they are looking for can only be found inside themselves, they search for a way in. What they will encounter will represent one of these manifestations of three different qualities of understanding.

The most *superficial level, exoteric,* represents a *literal, concrete understanding* of what are teaching metaphors and parables. The actual experience and aims of the teaching have not yet been experienced, but only captured conceptually. Recommendations are followed by rote, often assuming that the rote following of a practice, alone, will bring what is sought. This is the level of the technician who has learned methods but may not yet have the deepest understanding of what the method can lead to.

In the *middle* is the *mesoteric level*. Here there is real information and help from the esoteric level and a perspective that supports the practice of these inner truths and suggestions from the esoteric. Understanding is only partial, but genuine and growing.

The deepest level, called *esoteric*, represents the perceptions of people whose understanding comes from *direct experience*. They understand the essence of the search because it is alive inside them. They are able to manifest from that deepest understanding.

Psychology: Modern and Ancient

At the *exoteric* level, contemporary psychotherapy orients towards reducing distressing symptoms and behaviors as quickly as possible. If *only* relieving stress and feeling happy is one's primary aim in life, then the training and schools at this level are very helpful in teaching how to live a more comfortable ordinary existence There is a focus on the interaction between types of thinking, social influences, and imbalance in the personality, but it does not include an awareness that personality is an artificial construct floating on the surface of a deeper ocean. It believes that personality is the acme of the inner world. It does not recognize or work towards bringing a person deeper into their *existential* realm, but, rather, to help them be more comfortable and productive in their normal life and environment at the exoteric level. Even with this limited surface goal, it has become very helpful in this regard, reducing the suffering of millions, and teaching them techniques to maintain themselves on a healthier level.

A *mesoteric* oriented therapy shows how to begin *separating the sense of oneself* from the behavioral and psychological manifestations emanating *from* personality and how to rebalance one's physical, emotional, and intellectual energies. The idea of hidden information in our minds that shape our lives ... but of which we are not aware ... the "unconscious" or "shadow" side of our mysterious psyche ... is explored through the ancient art of dreams and free association. The creative energy within us is allowed to emerge and play a role in shaping the direction of the therapy. It is assumed that insight can relieve symptoms This is a movement towards a stage of consciousness that some call *individuation*. In moments when this separation of identification with personality occurs, the increase in sensitivity may allow for reception of the essence of the *esoteric* understanding deeper within.

Although identically formulated techniques are often used across therapies, and the levels can blur around these boundaries, the quality of understanding behind their application will create very different possibilities. A therapist cannot guide deeper than they themselves have traveled. The person seeking help for their distress may not be functioning at, or even yet developed to, a level of consciousness that would allow for access to deeper regions.

At the *Esoteric* level focus emerges on a *transpersonal* perspective. Who am I beyond the construction of personality? As I approach the living of this question, I begin to experience myself from beyond my personality, perhaps even beyond my sense of individuality. I enter a new world of perspective and understanding which can only be experienced from this new location within/beyond myself.

This esoteric level seems to have existed in the earliest history of humankind and its understanding transmitted from one generation to the next *experientially* by those who had, themselves, been initiated into the reality of the mystery. Today it partially continues to exist, in what are called *transformational therapies*, concerned with discovering our essential nature buried beneath acquired personality. It provides a way of working with what appears on the other side of this inner doorway. The primary aim of these therapies is not the immediate cessation of suffering without understanding the root and meaning of the suffering, but rather to discover how to heal the deeper wound between the conditioned personality identifying itself with its material body and life interests ... and our deeper nature as a spiritualized energy confused to find itself dwelling within a body ... but without any understanding of how it came to be or what role it is designed to play during its existence on Earth.

The Golden Rule and Transformation of Being

"And as ye would that men should do to you, do ye also to them likewise." – Christianity

"Do naught unto others which would cause you pain if done to you." – Hindu

"Do not do to others what you do not want them to do to you" – Confucius

"Talk to each as to neither humble nor distress" – Sufi

"Thou shalt love thy neighbor as thyself." – Hebrew

The most ancient of principles that binds all religious and philosophical traditions together into one fabric is what we have come to call "The Golden Rule." Simple in its statement, its actual practice seems at best fitful and, for many, difficult to impossible from the level of our ordinary consciousness. Were it not so, the advice would not need to be repeated in endless variations, to all peoples, for thousands of years.

The Sages urge us to find a way and offer practical guidance, but in trying the actual consistent application of the principle, we discover that what sounds simple is beset by a gauntlet of roadblocks. To be able to practice the principle with those we already love is not always easy. To practice it with others with whom such affection is absent is something else.

The communal benefits of consistent, fair, and kind behavior with one's neighbors is an obvious foundational skill for building any sustainable, creative community. But this ancient urging is not only about my relationship with others. It is also about my relationship with myself. If we are honest, we must admit that the interference patterns reside within ourselves.

There are levels of practice. Being, at minimum, polite to others outwardly is only half the equation. Often my inner attitude is far less generous. If I am only practicing outside, what is happening in my interior?

Two personal examples come to mind. A few years ago, I was walking through a local park. Off to the far right, my peripheral vision picked up a figure moving in my direction. I saw, arising spontaneously in my mind, judgmental assessments about this figure even before I realized what was being reacted to. On watching this inner reaction, I realized assumptions were automatically being made about this person based on their physical appearance and clothing. Although in actual interaction with such people, I was always courteous, and if needed, helpful, there was, to my surprise, a disconnect with inner attitudes. As I watched this unpleasant manifestation in my psychological interior, I saw it as the assuming part of myself that has become mechanical in its reactions. I had to admit that these types of attitudes were expressions I would disapprove of when manifested by others.

Recently I was listening to a research-author read his book about exploring drug-induced mystical experiences. I noticed my feeling of impatience and astonishment at the disconnect between the personal dramatic experiences he was describing and his intellectual incapacity to recognize their significance in terms of a deeper reality. He spoke the words, but his tone suggested a continuing intellectual distancing from his feelings. I became interested in the emotional strength of my annoyance until I recognized that I was reacting to a very similar part of myself. My inner "Doubting Thomas" hid his skepticism behind a cloak of scientific objectivity to avoid confronting his own fear of letting go of his rigid world view.

How would I want others to think and feel about me in their interior psychological world?

I would not want them making private judgments about me even while playing the role of the Golden Rule towards me outwardly. If this is so, then I have to learn to practice treating others as I would wish them to treat me in the privacy of my heart and mind as well as outwardly in manifested behavior.

The Golden principle encourages an experience of the blending of I and Thou. What type of "I," what aspect or level of myself can I bring to this sharing of goodwill? To love you as I love myself would first require that I do, actually, love myself and with the appropriate quality of what we call "love." If I don't love myself, what love do I have to give to you? If my self-love is narcissistic, I am blind to you. If the self I love is my self-image, constructed out of personality, then my understanding of you will be distorted by my need to protect and enhance my image of myself in your eyes. In that case, I will do unto you what I believe will cause you to feel good about me. To be objective about what you need, I would have to be objective about myself.

To be objective about myself I would have to know both my subjectivity and what can objectively observe it. To know myself at this level would require that I recognize that I am made of levels, some capable to striving for a state worthy of the Golden Rule and many others disinterested, oblivious or hostile to it. If I recognize these levels in me, I can recognize them in others.

The intimacy of experiencing a state, a level of consciousness, that can hold the taste of I-Thou, can also bring sufficient objectivity such that I can sense my level and the level in that moment of the Other. At times, a true application of the Golden Rule may necessitate direct honesty, not polite pieties or avoidance, but also a sensitivity to timing and location so as to "neither humble nor distress".

The universal key to this mystery has also come down to us from antiquity:

"Know Thyself".
"Let who is without sin cast the first stone".
"On the way to enlightenment, one must swallow everything said about another".

Days of fasting and self-reflection, confession to oneself or another, are included in all traditions to open the door to this process. These practices are clearly suggestions for preparation to achieve a state of inner understanding which would allow for the consistent application of the Golden Rule. Such consistent application, when manifested by others, catches our attention, and we look towards such individuals as models and verification that the practice is possible.

I believe the practice of this principle is difficult because the understanding of its purpose is often too shallow. Its potential is far deeper than the practical challenge of living in communities with minimum interpersonal conflict, and it is too easily confused with being "nice," a "good" person, which belong to a level of reason that dances with the danger of inflated self-image and the insufficiency of role-playing rather than an actual transformation in Being.

In fact, The Golden Rule can be understood as a practice designed to transform one into a person who is capable of consistently manifesting its principles because of a change in understanding of oneself. How can I put myself into the shoes of another if I am unaware of standing in similar shoes within myself? To do this requires that I am aware of my own suffering, my own errors of judgment, my own hypocrisies, my own weaknesses, and failings ... all the manifestations I use to justify my lack of acceptance of those who display these qualities I would not want to attribute to myself. How can I understand and have compassion for the weaknesses, unpleasant manifestations, and suffering of others if I do not understand and have compassion for my own weaknesses, unpleasant manifestations, and sufferings?

It is my refusal to acknowledge traits, unbecoming to the image I want to have of myself, that blinds me to the parts of me that I judge in others. Judging these unattractive qualities in others helps me to distance from them in myself. This creates blockages in my psychological world that dull my sensitivity, my compassion, my willingness, or actual capacity to try to understand the position of another, particularly when it clashes with my own values and beliefs about myself.

G.I. Gurdjieff, philosopher, mystic, and teacher of the first half of the 20th century, also presents versions of the Golden Rule in his teachings, culminating in a responsibility for universal relationship, "Love everything that breathes," as the culmination of such a practice.

But wishing does not make it so. The price to be paid for the development of this capacity is a prolonged period in the purgatorial state of staying present to the discontinuity between my wish to be able to fulfill this commandment and my personal incapacity to do so, due to the many attitudes and prejudices conditioned into my psychology by my surrounding social structure. Gurdjieff calls this state of active remorse, *Divine*. The fire of its experience is necessary to develop the quality of objective, self-reflective responsibility that can lead to an objective, honest and forgiving relationship with myself. From that foundation, the differences between myself and others disappear. Just like me, they hope and wish and suffer. And just like me, everyone I lay eyes upon will die.

If I allow myself to feel this truth, my heart will break with tenderness for all.*

---

* This essay first appeared in *Parabola Magazine*: Society for Myth and Tradition, NY , Winter 2021-22

Breath and the Practice of Letting Go

One of my favorite teaching stories relates the tale of an old monk and his young novice walking over hill and dale to visit another monastery. At a river crossing, they meet a young woman with a heavy bundle who is afraid to ford the stream. She asks the monks for help. The young monk is momentarily paralyzed by the request, but the old monk immediately agrees and lifts her in his arms and carries her across where he puts her down, accepts her thanks, and begins to walk on, allowing the younger man to bring the woman's bundles across. The young monk rushes to catch up with him and walks behind for several miles lost in reaction. Finally, he stops and demands of his elder, "We are told never to touch women. How could you break our rule?" The elder looks at him a moment and replies, "I put her down hours ago. How long are you going to carry her?"

"Let go" is a recommendation often suggested to solve the problem of identification, a contemporary version of the traditional religious admonition, "Let go and let God".

Theologian Reinhold Niebuhr authored this advice which has come to be known as the Serenity Prayer used in Alcoholics Anonymous: "God give me the serenity to accept things which cannot be changed. Give me courage to change things which must be changed, and the wisdom to tell the difference."

What is it we are to "let go" of? Obviously, useless worry and rigid adherence to rules in situations where they should not apply, are two examples reflected above. Gurdjieff goes much further in his recommendation, stating that it is our addiction to self-image, our interpretation of meaning, and our reactions conditioned into us by life which we must abandon. He states that it is our mistaken belief in who and what we imagine we are which lies at the heart of unnecessary suffering. His recommendations for this transformation, can be seen as an ongoing discipline captured in the injunctions: "Try to remember yourself always and everywhere", "Man cannot do" and "Die to yourself before you die".

Early Steps in Letting Go

How to accomplish the shift to "letting go" in the face of a weak attention, continually attracted by the gravitational pull of *"identification"* and *"inner considering"*?* Traditional recommendations focus on an intellectual shift of viewpoint to alter emotions of frustration, despair, and resentment, i.e. "Just let it go", "Get over it". "Drop it". "You just need an attitude adjustment". Many people find this a difficult transition to make.

In my experience, Gurdjieff provides the missing piece to this puzzle and brings it into the realm of a practical possibility by suggesting we begin with studying the sensations of our body. His foundational training in dividing attention and sensing the physical body can lead to a transformation in perspective. What I have found in my practice is an *experiential* recognition that I am not my body but rather *an awareness inside a body*. This experience provides a ground to which attention can be returned as an aid to breaking a state of identification in the *moment*. Once established, this capacity can provide a foundation for other interesting explorations which further facilitate the weakening of identification.

The Breath

Focus on the breath is common in many systems of transformation. Unlike many other traditions, however, Gurdjieff warns *against* breath manipulation, but rather recommends a practice of watching and sensing the natural rhythms of one's breathing.

When I was first introduced to the idea of just *watching* my breath, I found myself frustrated and dismayed by my initial attempts. Whenever

---

* *Identification: Gurdjieff's term for the state of conscientiousness in which attention is so absorbed in its perception that the sense of oneself as the person, in your body, at that moment, having this experience, vanishes. Without this level of self-awareness, one is vulnerable to becoming captive of one's conditioned and mechanical reactions and patterns. There is no capacity for individual discernment or decision making because the individual has disappeared from their own awareness and been replaced by mechanical reactions we call "personality". This process also typically occurs outside the individual's awareness leaving one in a semi-hypnotic state while believing one is fully conscious.*

Inner considering: Gurdjieff's term for being concerned with what others think about us, especially to the extent to which we project our beliefs about what others believe about us onto them without realizing that it is our own opinion of ourself that we worry others believe about us.

I remembered to bring attention to my breath…its rhythm changed. It was as if my breath became self-conscious about being watched. For a long while, every attempt brought the same result. I was certainly able to feel the movement, but I wanted to be able to study it without causing it to change.

I persisted in trying to catch a glimpse of my breath without the breath noticing it was being looked at. At some point, it finally relaxed its re-action to my gaze and did not alter its rhythm when touched by my intentionally directed attention. It has never been an issue since.

This led to some interesting experiences. I noticed that there are four parts to the breath, not just inhalation and exhalation. There are pauses at the top and bottom of the cycle. I became very interested in these two additional points. I tried counting to see if I could predict when the breath would release and when it would engage again and realized this was not always predictable. There were fraction-of-a-second differences between my estimate and the reality. How did the breath know when to start and stop? I can intentionally manipulate it, but when left alone, it has a life of its own that does not require my consultation.

I also noticed, as all meditators learn, that when meditation deepens, the breath slows down. Sometimes it slows to only a few, barely percep-tible breaths per minute. This change is involuntary. Here also, I noticed the breathing slowed and sped up on its own without my input.

As I became more comfortable and accomplished in this study, I rec-ognized that *I was not doing the breathing* … but rather *my body was breathing* … and that the more I let go of trying to control or influence my breath, the more clearly I could observe it.

Resting part of my attention gently on the breath became another way of using the impression of being inside a body, with its own rhythms, its own life, to truly *experience* … *not just realize* … I was not in control of this process. It is one thing to intellectually know this is true, but entirely different to *experience* the truth of it. But I am not going to sit in medi-tation all day. To study it during normal life activities requires letting go of attempts to manipulate it in any way.

In time, another discovery appeared. Typically, when attending to the breath, I would begin with the inhalation and consider the expiration the completion. In .... Out ... In ... Out ... I could visualize oxygen molecules coming in and undigestible carbon dioxide exiting my aerating filtration system. Then, I reversed the pattern by shifting attention to the exhalation first and then the inhalation. Out ... In ... Out ... In. There appeared a distinct sensation of something moving into the interior of my body on the exhalation. Not only was carbon dioxide being projected out of my body back into the air, but something else was entering the interior of my body, like some part of air that was retained. Subtle at first, this impression solidified with practice. There was now the distinct impression of an *energizing something* flowing into my body, feeding it, as unusable air exited on the exhalation. Was I experiencing the movement of oxygen into my blood stream to be carried to each of my billions of cells? I seemed to be experiencing the digestion of air.

It is said that on average, we take 22,000 breaths a day, from birth to death. How many breaths am I aware of each day? I am clearly not in charge of this process. If my breathing were powered by the gaze of my attention, I would suffocate quickly. Evidently, my body's processes do not require my subjective awareness. My life is sustained by the living mechanism which I continually rediscover myself dwelling within.

The Voice

To facilitate developing awareness of the constant involuntary breathing of my body, it was also suggested to practice being present to my voice. As I attempted to do so, this brought a surprising experience.

An aspect of breathing is the ability to make sounds as air passes outward from lungs through the shaping instruments of larynx, mouth, tongue, teeth, lips, and air pressure. As with the breath itself, we are typically oblivious to the mystery of how the voice speaks for us.

I vividly recall a fascinating moment in front of a classroom of students. I had been hired by the local university to teach a course on stress management based on a book I had published on the topic. I walked into the first class and stood in front of a room of students. Just before I was about to begin, I recalled the recommendation of listening to my voice. I shifted part of my attention to my chest and throat. I noticed the students watching me in anticipation of my beginning. I was trying also to "let go", to try and watch and listen to what came from my mouth. As I continued to watch myself, I began to wonder when my voice would speak. As I thought about my opening remarks, I realized with surprise ... and then discomfort, that I ... actually ... had ... no ...idea ... how words translated from my head and through my vocal cords to fill my mouth with meaningful sounds. As the students stared at me, I stared at myself, mute in front of them. I began to think that I might have to announce that I wasn't feeling well and dismiss the class ... except I didn't know how to speak those words.

I had spoken all my life, but now, trying to watch the process from a bit of distance, I realized that I did not actually know how I made words appear in my own mouth... most of the time it just happened, automatically, mechanically, often without my initiation. Sometimes when I tried to express feelings or ideas with intention, the words or tone did not convey what I had wished.

Staying present to my voice has been a long and interesting practice. Typically, one's awareness of oneself disappears when one speaks. It is very difficult to listen to one's own voice in the moment, including intonation and accompanying body gestures... but it is possible. For a long time, I became frustrated that I could not hold my position and listen at the same time. The frustration increased my identification even more.

After a time, I looked for another approach, ... a change in perspective. I told myself, "Relax. Don't try so hard. Change your attitude from "I *must* do this ...now! Permanently! What is wrong with me?" ... to ... "How interesting that part of me wants to listen but is unable to sustain the effort without forgetting." I now accept that I won't be able to stay awake to this aim for long, so I don't expect to. I just try to stay present to myself and my voice ... when I remember. Instead of "I must stay awake", I changed my attitude to "How long can I be aware of my voice this time before falling again into the sleep of forgetfulness? One second? Two? Five?" Next time I wake up, I make another bet with myself. "Last time, I lasted maybe a second. Let me try for two seconds this time and see what happens." Eventually, this task became a fun and interesting game between me and myself."

At times when I knew I would have something to say, I practiced it in my mind while listening to the voice in my head. Then I would say it aloud. I tried this first when alone so I wouldn't be captured by inner considering ... what I feared others would think of me. Then I discovered reading out loud to myself and I would listen to my voice read. I talked aloud to myself while looking into a mirror ... then practiced while reading aloud to someone else. Then I tried giving a speech, or just talking aloud with someone while practicing again and again, waking up and trying again and again.

To become a human who has transformed into a person who is not always controlled by their conditioning, one must separate the *observing* part from the *reacting* part. This journey begins with separating one's sense of identity from the body that one inhabits. Many traditions have various methods for achieving this. Recognition that I am not in *direct* control of the manifestations of my body, *experientially* drives home the point that there is a much deeper mystery to my nature than I had imagined.

Gurdjieff's teaching and other esoteric traditions speak of the necessity to "die to oneself" before the body dies. This requires, among other efforts, *letting go* of my fear and greed-based desires. Such fears and desires compel me to either try to influence ... or even force ... others to be and to behave as I wish them to. They may even drive me to force changes in my nature that don't conform to my idealized self-image, which was constructed in me as a result of those very fears and desires. I will eventually have to let go of cherished ideas of who and what I am ... let go of blind acceptance of what I have been told to believe.

An initial aspect of this preparation can begin with the discovery that my breath and voice function autonomously. I don't breathe! The *body breathes* for me. I don't speak. The voice translates what my mind wishes to communicate. I can change the words by thinking of different ones, but there is a space between the thoughts and their expression through the voice. It is a space I have never been able to see into. Perhaps, dear Reader, you would like to make this discovery for yourself? What questions might it raise about what and who you believe you are if you verified this initial step in the process of psychological transformation?

To conclude the story of the tongue-tied professor ... finally, I searched my memory for things I had said in the introduction to the book which might fit this circumstance. Clumsily, my voice began to make a scratchy sound ... then a fumbling sentence about my aims for the course dribbled out in an awkward manner. At that point, the voice took off smoothly and began to mechanically address the subject while I listened to it along with the class.

A few days later, I shared this experience with my mentor. He smiled in gentle amusement and recognition. "The initial shock can be like that", he offered. "Don't be concerned. You will get used to it." In fact, this vocal paralysis never happened again ... but to this moment I am still amazed that my life sustaining breath, and my primary source of communication, have a life of their own to which I am privy only at the margins.

Wish, Meaning, Aim

I was in conversation with an old friend recently. We were reflecting on our combined nearly 150 years of living experiences. What had we come to? He initially stated that he wasn't sure that life had any meaning, in the philosophical or spiritual sense. I demurred. My sense was very different. My end of the ensuing conversation went something like this.

"OK. Let's look at the materialistic viewpoint. Materialists believe the Universe and everything in it has unfolded through a series of random events, up to and including life on Earth, animal, human ...and oneself, in particular. It has no inherent meaning in itself. Therefore, my personal existence and that of all those I care about are also without meaning ... except what is imagined by the participants in this random, accidental Universe."

But ... if this *is* your viewpoint ... are you comfortable with it? Are you disappointed or concerned that you cannot discover a sense of meaning? Does life seem full or does there occasionally feel to be something missing? If you cannot find meaning in Life, in existence, in a relationship, in an interesting search or adventure ... do you wish you could? If your answer is yes, then your wish and search *has meaning ... for you.*

This begs the question: in a meaningless, random, accidental Universe ... how do we account for the *meaningful experiences* of a living creature that is a part of the Universe ... a creature that experiences wishes, that conceptualizes *aims* and experiences differing subjective interpretations of things depending on the *meaning* of an event for those experiencing it?

A dictionary definition: *A wish is a desire, a feeling or longing for something to happen or be done: a feeling of wanting to do or have something ... an act of thinking about something that you want and hoping that you may achieve.*

This phenomenon is so deeply embedded that our language has the phrase, "Wishing makes it so." Although this saying is often incorrect, it does have a basis in observed fact.

A wish sets a direction which eliminates some possibilities and increases odds for those which lie in the direction of the wish. The intensity of the wish, the degree to which one's "heart is set on it", determines the strength of the drive and can power a laser focus on the goal which cuts through inevitable distractions. How close one gets to the idealized goal depends on talent, support, and luck ... although a strong wish can increase chances of a fortuitous outcome.

When the "heart" connects intent with capacity, energy appears. The strength of this concept is reflected in the long list of synonyms for the experience of wishing. For example: "desire hope crave pine whim aspiration", to name only a few.

A wish is focused on a hoped-for future that does not yet exist. Its interest lies outside the time and space of the wisher in the higher realm of possibility.

That future must have meaning for the aspirant or there would be no wish. Why make the effort to wish for something not yet in existence unless it is important to you ... has meaning for you?

The implication of the ancient adage, "as above, so below", is that the existence of the psychic phenomenon of wishing, at our human level of the Universe, must have its reflection at other levels as well.

If something exists anywhere, then its existence is a fact. Since the capacity to wish for something of meaning and significance exists in humans ... and humans are made of and are part of the materials and energies of the Universe ... then the Universe contains organic life forms for whom the search for meaning is the meaning of their lives.

Thus, the reality of a wish and the capacity for seeking and maintaining an aim, is *itself* proof of the existence of meaning in the Universe.

Whether we discover intelligent life on other planets, we can confirm that life does exist in the Universe from our one sample of the planet Earth. The exception proves the rule.

And ... what could it mean that the life form, *Human*, has the capability to look into a future that does not exist and by wishing that it might come to pass, may alter events in such a way as to bring that future hope into a materialized reality when the moment presents itself? Is it meaningful to you, dear Reader, that you too have this capacity to shape events through time?

Why would humans have this capacity to wish and the desire for meaning if it is not built into our psychological architecture? Why would we have evolved to search for something that does not exist?

I would argue that life forms evolve to exist in their given environment. If meaning were not an inherent part of our universal environment, we would not have the impulse for search. Whether one wants to make this acknowledgement and undertake the journey is a personal choice. One who chooses not to search cannot rationally declare that what they refuse to acknowledge does not exist. It may not exist for them, but it certainly does for others.

As Inside, So Outside; As Above, So Below

The Heart of the Matter

I was visiting Zion National Park in Utah with my wife and another couple. I wanted to explore a side canyon on foot, but my companions were either not interested in, or physically incapable of, joining me. As I set off on my walk without them, I became aware of a tension in my chest and a conflicted dialogue in my mind.

On the one hand, I felt it would be unfair for me to be away from the group for too long. As I continued to move deeper into the intriguing narrow canyon, I was also following the mental dialogue which I recognized as both a cause of, and a reflection of, my state of emotional tension. How to differentiate appropriate consideration for my companions from the neurotic *inner considering* ... the concern that others may think of you the way you think and feel about yourself ..., which had developed in me as a defense, since boyhood, against disapproval, with its primary manifestation being self-sacrifice?

On the other hand, my love of the Western United States, which appeared in my mid-twenties during my brief time living in that area, had been a source of frustration over the subsequent fifty years of self-imposed exile in the East due to feelings of obligations to family ties, an established clinical practice that could not be easily transferred to a different location, as well as the financial responsibilities of supporting a family and raising children. A couple of rare trips to the West continually revived my longing to spend time in that vast landscape but left me with a feeling of being trapped by the current structure of my life. During these few trips, I was typically with family members whose desire to explore did not match my own, so I always deferred to others and turned away from side explorations I could make individually.

Now, here I was again in the same situation. This time, with the assent of my companions, I asserted my personal wish to not repeat this pattern. Nevertheless, as I set out, the above-mentioned tension and inner dialogue began to rise. I did not know how long it would take me to complete the round trip to the canyon head. How long would they have to wait for me? Was this "fair" to them? Was I being "selfish". These doubts were met by a counterargument that I had sacrificed my interests for the real, or imagined, convenience of others for far too long.

I noticed that my walking was pressured, not relaxed. My body was moving faster than usual. I saw the thought accompanying this atypical movement reflected a compromise to satisfy both arguments: I could complete my self-appointed mission in the shortest time, so as to mini-mize their waiting for my return. I also realized that I had not intentionally initiated this compromise, but rather discovered it after noticing the increase in walking speed. Something other than the part of my mind engaged in the dialogue had made this decision for me.

I now became as interested in this inner tension as I was fascinated by the spectacular scenery outside. Besides the mechanical quality of the di-alogue and my body's solution, I could also feel the taste of tenacity and determination to push through this life-long internal pattern.

At that moment I began to wonder about the quality of *Will* being brought to bear on the situation. My body was uncomfortable at this un-usual speed, but it persisted at its designated pace. Why, I wondered, was I behaving differently in this situation than I had in the previous exam-ples? Why, this time, was I breaking with my pattern?

Where was this steady application of Will coming from? I had always assumed that Will originated in the frontal lobes of my brain, making choices, giving orders to the body and insisting on the mind's wish in the face of objections from other parts of myself. Now I recognized an additional, critical, perhaps primary, component.

When faced with choices, how is one selected over another? I saw, in this case, what was driving me onward was a determination coming from my *feelings*. I *wanted* this experience. I wanted it more than my need to please. I wanted this experience strongly enough to leave my party for an unknown period of time; but there was insufficient force to intentionally slow my speed and take as much time as I wanted: so, I could not help myself from driving my body at an uncomfort-able pace.

My goal was to reach the canyon's terminus so I wouldn't have to spend the rest of my life wondering what lay at its end. Something in me had found a compromise. Yet, the extent of my inner considering, my conditioned life-long concern about not displeasing others, required my body to suffer in order to accomplish this balancing act. Thus, the total experience was a mixture of pain as well as pleasure.

This got me reflecting on the role of emotion in an act of Will. There is certainly the will of the body to survive and seek comfort and pleasure. This is built into the design of the survival mechanism. There is the will directed from the frontal lobes of the brain, a will which can select what to give attention to and then maintain its focus on the subject of choice ... a will sufficient to bring attention back repeatedly as it starts to drift. There is the quality of will which can choose and maintain course in the face of extreme obstacles, going against the will of the body and even one's emotional resistance ... or sometimes even knowingly against one's "better judgement".

As my body continued moving me deeper into the canyon, I became curious as to the location of the will-of-the-moment driving me forward against the friction of my conflicted inner state. My body was obviously uncomfortable at the pace which another part of me was driving to maintain it. My intellect was so occupied with this question of levels that remembering to look at the scenery required additional effort. My ordinary mind was producing an intermittent dialogue about this old inner friction while another part was listening and engaging in the observing of this pattern as described above. What was the role of my feelings in this interesting situation? There was a sense of longing and determination in the center of my chest. I could see clearly that the driving motive in this moment was this combination of *desire* and *perseverance*. The decision was not only intellectual, but heartfelt because "I had my heart set on it".

The power of feelings or values or principles can be more potent than reason or bodily preferences for comfort and safety. I reflected on the wisdom of our language in this regard. "The heart is forever making the head its fool." "Beauty is not in the face; Beauty is a light in the heart." "Wherever you go, go with all your heart." "One of the hardest things in life is having words in your heart that you can't utter." "If only ... the desire of your mind should become the desire of your heart".

I could see how my conditioning had often made me "faint of heart" when it came to asserting what was important to me. I realized that "If there is a will, there is a way" involves three different flavors of "Will". When the mind, body and heart are of "like mind", "one mind", the melding motivations create a force of great power. When these three containers of Will are in conflict, we become ambivalent, inconstant, clumsy in execution, and give conflicting messages to ourselves and others.

A new question arose for me. At any moment of engagement, with others, my environment or myself, where is the seat of my Will? Are all three of my functional aspects, mind, body, and feelings coordinated or fractured? When noticing that I am conflicted, of two minds (or more) around a choice, clarifying where within my triadic nature the resistance lies can turn this type of internal friction into a source of interest and deepening understanding of my multi-layered nature.

Since that moment of insight, my heart has been in the pursuit of this question as I recognize it as "the heart of the matter".

Communication

I was walking along a forest trail, while listening to Gurdjieff's luminous music through my headphones. I have always been deeply moved by his melodies and rhythms. I find them evocative of deep, strange, wonderful feelings and images of what, I visualize, were scenes and experiences he had as a youth, wandering through Asia and the Middle East.

What I realized, almost instantly, was not a new thought for me, but it had an *emotional* and *sensory* depth which elevated the moment to a state of epiphany. What I now *felt* and *saw*, not only theorized, was the nature of the process happening *within* me in the moment.

Through the vibrations resonating from the headphones ... to my eardrums ... to the tiny bones inside my ear ... to the even tinier hairs on the tiny bones ... to the adjacent auditory nerves ... to the parts of my brain that would process the sounds and stimulate the feelings and ... perhaps create resonant images...I, the audience, somewhere in my mind, would *experience* ... across years and continents, a taste of Gurdjieff's impressions and feelings. Our minds...his long dead... and mine... receiving his message just now... on another continent... in another century... were for this moment entwined. His electronically preserved 'mind-footprints' were playing upon the neurons *in my brain* to reproduce an electromagnetic field to aproximate the one in *his mind* when he was producing the music for *this person ... me ...* whom he would never meet, but hoped would be a kindred soul.

Here was the mystical and miraculous phenomenon of communication ... the two sources, sending and receiving were now sharing a common space, a common sense.

From the dictionary: as a noun: to communicate is a process by which information is exchanged between individuals through a common system of symbols, signs, or behavior ... a means of sending or receiving information, such as phone lines or computers "satellite communications" as a verb: *to "commune" with somebody/something, to share your emotions and feelings with someone or something without speaking; to be in close spiritual contact with someone or something* From (12c.), from Medieval Latin *"communia"* ... *"that which is common*".

Minds interpenetrate at a distance, both in space and time. How astonishing! Libraries are filled with symbolic representations of the thoughts, feelings, experiences, transferred from the perishable organic brain of the authors into symbols on a thin piece of wood or fiber we call paper... hoping that from time to time other minds, somewhere in the future, perhaps on the other side of the planet, will open themselves to their messages and invite them into their own experiential memory banks to live again ... in another time and place. What a stupendous, expo-nential increase in the capacity of minds to interpenetrate and change each other. For all of history prior, minds could only be transferred directly, individual to individual, through direct speech or contact. Now, the other person need not appear until a later time... perhaps not for cen-turies or millennia.

Today, information can be stored in the electric-magnetic field which envelopes the Earth. Anyone with a small communication device in hand can access this global library, communicate, and contribute to it and download from it the words, thoughts, feelings, images of millions of others.

But ... do we appreciate the deeper mystery underlying this process? To say that we have created a global brain focuses on our technological cleverness. But ... we *have created a global brain!* This electromag-netic field of information encompasses the planet through its atmos-phere in which every life form is saturated with these waves. This is now a new part of the Earth **...** and *each of us as part of the Earth ourselves.*

Does this imply that the Earth, itself, is waking up? The planet already generates from itself ... and is saturated by... electromagnetic impulses from the sun, the planets, and its own interior core. Now humanity has added a new vibration. Is the Earth listening... or is this the Earth speaking?

We seem to be sharing our collective minds such that the information permeates the planet and radiates outward into the space beyond. Listened to from afar, it would sound like the planet was talking.

If someone, far away was listening and decoding, the collective mind of humanity would be uploaded into the collective mind of the listener circling another star in the incommensurable distances of space.

How remarkable ... both this idea ... and that it was stimulated by the sounds transmitting information from the mind of Gurdjieff to the mind of his composer, de Hartmann ... and now, over a century later into my mind and leading it to the thoughts above which I am now sharing with you, dear Reader. How remarkable.

As Inside, So Outside; As Above, So Below

The Quantum Nature of Relationship Entanglement

It had been three or four days since, Susan, my wife of twenty years, had died. My memory begins as I approached our house from our stand-alone garage. I had obviously just gotten out of the car, but I don't remember where I had been. It was dusk. The house was dark. It was never dark when she was home, only when we came home together at night. I paused and looked at it. The windows looked like blank eyes. The house *felt* empty ... lifeless ... dead! It was as if the house had been alive and now it was no longer. It was a very strange emotion ... like another dimension of feeling had suddenly opened up. Experience had ... expanded.

I entered the house. It was cold as well as dark. The experience, the smell, taste and feel of emptiness intensified. She wasn't there. Where was she? Where did she go? How could she have been here and now she wasn't here anymore ... nevermore?

I saw an image appear in my mind of a hole in the center of my torso. Yes ... that was accurate. I felt gutted, as if a huge piece of me had been ripped out, leaving in its place a gaping hole. This was not just an idea or an image. I *felt* it. There was an empty place in my center!

I knew this as part of grief from earlier experiences in this excruciating state. A part of me, somehow, was actually missing. *Something* of each of the two of us had, literally, become blended over two decades. When she died, her part of that something seemed to have left with her.

I saw another image appear in my mind. As with many images in dreams, on awakening they can still be seen and understood for a short while but cannot fit into the limitation of words. It was like that with this image. The meaning of the image was to show me ... even now I still see it and understand it but am struggling to find the words to talk about its implications.

What is the underlying nature of the *energetic bond* we call relationship? What is "liking", "caring", "loving"? What exactly gets *entangled* when we form an emotional *bond* with someone? This *something* feels to both contain and carry us ... along with another passenger who comes into our psychological-emotional space.

What Can Science Tell Us?

Research into the role of the physical heart and its relationship to our other functions, is in its infancy. The science mentioned in this exploration will require replication and validation by additional sources, particularly as its implications suggest a paradigm shift. However, there is an interesting co-relation between what religious and philosophical thinkers have posited for millennia and the new findings of *neuro-cardiology*.

Historically, philosophical and spiritual thought has long considered that the heart is the location of both emotion and reason. Aristotle believed it more important in this respect than the brain. A quote from Abu Nasr al-Frabi in the ninth century stated, "The ruling organ in the human body is the heart; the brain is a secondary ruling organ subordinated to the heart." Two centuries ago, French philosopher Auguste Comte said the brain should serve the heart. Twelfth century Christian mystic, Hildegard of Bingen, said, "The soul sits at the center of the heart, as though in a house." A contemporary researcher at the HeartMath Institute in California, Rollin McCraty Ph.D. says, "The most common denominator in all religions is that the heart is the seat of wisdom,"

In modern times, with the explosion of understanding about the structure and functions of the brain in our skull, it may be easy to assume that these older views of the heart as a seat of wisdom represent poetic hypotheses made by people who did not have the benefit of modern brain research. But recent discoveries in the new field of neuro-cardiology are re-evaluating this older viewpoint. The discovery of a bundle of 40 thousand specialized neurons in the heart, the *Intrinsic Cardiac Afferent Neurons*, or *Intracardiac Nervous System*, has been nicknamed the "heart's little brain." It forms a communication network within the heart that performs many of the same functions that are found in the brain.

Researchers at the HeartMath Institute state that the "heart communicates with the brain as much, if not more, than the reverse and does so by producing its own neurotransmitters and proteins similar to those found in the brain proper." They report research which suggests the heart's "brain" does this by converting the language of the body and emotions into electrical impulses … the language of the nervous system … and sending these signals to the brain in our head. The heart's coded messages tell the head brain when to adjust adrenaline levels in a stressful situation or when adrenaline is not required or when to release relaxation or pleasure hormones or how to focus on building a stronger immune system. "It has become clear in recent years that a sophisticated two-way communication occurs between the heart and the brain, with each influencing the other's function."*

The, now, frequent use of heart transplant surgery has disclosed something unexpected and controversial. There are anecdotal reports that some transplant recipients seem to be 'inheriting' memories from their heart donor's life, including changes in tastes, in personality and even emotional memories. Skepticism is appropriate in the face of paradigm-shifting evidence. Conventional explanations center around post-surgical stress or reactions to medication designed to reduce organ rejection. Other researchers are wondering if we are seeing the result of "cellular memories" that arrive with the donor's tissues and then begin to influence the recipient.

In all living beings, cells appear to learn from their experiences, perhaps through a classical conditioning paradigm. For example, if our body were not constantly learning which microbes were helpful, benign, or harmful, we would never develop an immune system. The cases suggestive of memory transfer with some heart transplants, imply the possibility that personality traits and conditioned reactions may be stored in the heart as well as the head brain.

All this activity, coordination, modulation of bio-chemical activity is powered by electricity. Research has discovered that every living cell generates its own electromagnetic field (EM). Each of those tiny fields overlaps with its neighbors, forming increasingly large and complex interactions. Thus, all the cells of an organ combine to produce the EM field for that organ. Ultimately, all organs, tissues, bone, and blood combine to produce an EM field surrounding the entire body.

The largest by far of these biologically generated EM fields is produced by the heart. The cardiac field is reported to extend several feet beyond the body and measurable by instrumentation. The heart's electrical field is reported to be about 60 times greater in amplitude than the electrical activity generated by the brain and 5000 times stronger. The heart

---

* *heartmath.org*

generates a continuous series of electromagnetic pulses in which the time interval between each beat varies in a dynamic and complex manner. Obviously, the heart's ever-present rhythmic field has a powerful influence on processes throughout the body.

The Heart-Math Institute reports that, when there is no disturbance, brain rhythms naturally synchronize with the heart's rhythmic activity. Also, during sustained feelings of love or appreciation, blood pressure and respiratory rhythms, among other oscillatory systems, harmonize to the heart's rhythm. Researchers report an ability to measure an exchange of "heart energy" between individuals up to 5 feet apart and that one person's brain waves can actually synchronize to another person's heart rhythm. In this way, there is reported evidence that the heart's electromagnetic field can transmit information between people. They report that individuals in a psycho-physiologically "coherent" state (synchronized) become more aware of the information encoded in the heart fields of those around them. This suggests possible connection with what we call intuition and empathy.

The field of psychosomatic medicine confirms that anger and intense grief can damage the heart. Research says we are statistically 20 times more likely to have a heart attack after the death of a loved one. "Broken heart syndrome" is the medical name for the condition we have always referred to as a "broken heart". The physiological changes induced by grief produce real pain and can mimic a heart attack. On the other hand, the heart, as well as the brain, can produce its own hormones like oxytocin, the "love" hormone and a "happy heart" experiences joy and contentment. The experience of a love-filled heart or a hard stone-cold heart or the excruciating pain of a broken heart, are exponentially worlds apart.

Happy hearts are reported to have coherent heart rhythms while the broken heart's rhythms are non-coherent. Some researchers in this field speculate that when we express emotions through expectorations like laughter, yelling, cheering, we may release chemicals and electromagnetic discharges reflecting these emotions.

"Coherence" is defined as a fixed relationship between the phase of waves in a beam of radiation of a single frequency. Two beams of light are coherent when the phase difference between their waves is constant; they are noncoherent if there is a random or changing phase relationship. Non-coherent waves produce interference patterns and can devolve into a chaotic state. Coherent light waves are normally stronger when compared to incoherent sources of light waves. Incoherent light waves are usually weaker. Coherent light waves are unidirectional. Incoherent light waves are omni-directional.*

I am also reminded of the well-established phenomena of *"personal space"*, a field around our body where most people report a preference for strangers to be 3-5 feet away from them to avoid an uncomfortable feeling that their space has been intruded upon. With more intimate relationships the space shrinks and touch and embrace are welcome. This is also how it is for me.

Dear Reader, if you are not experientially familiar with this phenomenon, try it for yourself with several people from intimates to strangers. How close can you come to them before you feel uncomfortable and want to stop or back up. What are you sensing to give you this information?

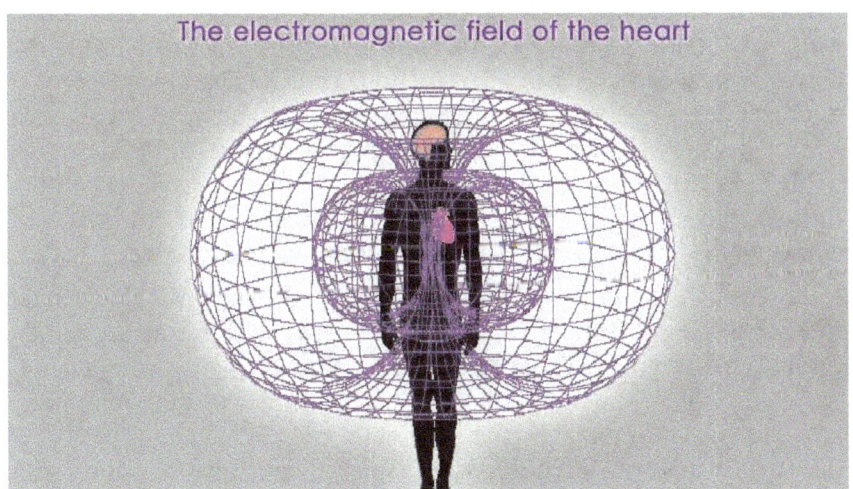

Image 5. "The Heart Has Its Own "Brain "and Consciousness"

With this background information, looking at an illustration of the heart's magnetic field is evocative. †

Implications

Every time the heart beats, it sustains an electromagnetic field which

---

* www.emedicalprep.com
† *Image by Rollin McCraty, Ph.D., Raymond Trevor Bradley, Ph.D. and Dana Tomasino, BA In 5D January 10, 2015 Meditation, Science,*

radiates within and outside the body. Researchers have historically considered that the mind is the center of human consciousness and theorized that mind phenomena result only from brain functions. Newly accumulating discoveries are pointing to the possibility that mind is a kind of "software" that extends beyond the limitations of our head. Professor Dan Siegel of UCLA School of Medicine describes the mind as, "the emergent self-organizing process, both embodied and relational, that regulates energy and information flow within and among us," ... and suggests that the mind extends outside our bodies.

The current Wikipedia entry of electromagnetic theories of consciousness proposes that "consciousness results when a brain produces an electromagnetic field with specific characteristics". Some electromagnetic theories are now considering that consciousness may be a quantum phenomenon.

There is yet another potential link in this question about the entanglement of emotions and electromagnetic fields. Electromagnetism is currently understood to be one of the four fundamental laws underlying the functioning of the universe. Everything in the Universe has its own EM field which expands, overlaps, and interacts with all the other EM fields in its neighborhood. The collective EM field of that neighborhood then interacts with EM fields from other neighborhoods. In this way, everything is interconnected with everything else in existence.

It is currently understood that the Earth generates its EM field from the rotation of its iron core. This EM field radiates outwards all around the Earth. Where it collides with the incoming flow of energy from the Sun, a standing shock wave is formed in the cavity between the ionosphere and Earth and vibrations emanating from the Earth's center. The area of the Earth's ionosphere between this Solar shock wave and the Earth, vibrates from this shock, creating an EM field. The frequency emitted by this shock is called the Schumann Resonance We can see manifestations of this field in the phenomenon we called Aurora Borealis.

The resonance of both these electromagnetic fields, the Earth and the atmosphere, correspond to the resonance frequencies of the EM fields of our body and brains. Because of this common resonance with each cell in our body and because this rhythmic pattern lies within the range of human electrical brainwaves, various authors have speculated that this aspect of the Earth's electromagnetic resonance field may act as a kind of global mind, with the capacity to organize and influence human consciousness. Less speculative is the growing appreciation that life, including us, has developed with the same frequency as the Earth and its surrounding heavens. and is a significant factor in the regulation of our health. Being "in tune" with Earth and Heaven seems to be what our natural state is designed to be ... a harmonic relationship. We are literally the children of the Earth and Sky, just as our ancient ancestors surmised.

There is a growing body of scientific studies suggesting that the Earth's magnetic field may influence and mediate DNA formation and our physical and mental health. Research reports that this resonance, the Schumann Resonance, was found to:

1. Restore or improve health in individuals living in an underground bunker (i.e., separated from the Earth-ionospheric resonance),

2. Led to speculation that the electromagnetic frequencies in the Earth-ionosphere cavity have played a governing role in the evolution of human and mammalian brainwave patterns, emotional distress and migraine headaches.

3. Using a weak electromagnetic field pulsing at 7 Hz (the Schumann Resonance) for 18 hours, DNA contained in a glass tube was reported to have transferred and been detectable in a second glass vial that originally had nothing in it but water. The researchers speculated that the 7 Hz played a substantial role in 'extracting' the DNA information from the one test tube and communicating it into the other test tube.

4. Two people in separate rooms were presented with identical magnetic fields at approximately 7 Hz. When one of these individuals drew a picture, the other person could roughly approximate that drawing, even though they were in a separate room.

Based on this information, there is growing concern that the proliferation of man-made electromagnetic fields has given rise to a kind of electromagnetic chaos that will damage all life.*

Resonance and Life

The magnetic resonance of the Earth and Ionosphere is in the same range as the electromagnetic resonance in our brains. The cells of our body also respond to this resonance and emit it back. Science is now discovering that every cell in the body creates an electromagnetic field.

---

* HeartMath Institute

All organs generate an EM field, the largest being the heart, emanations of which can be measured 3-5 feet away. Heart electrical rhythm effects electrical activity in the brain ... and vice versa. When these frequencies are coherent, functioning of heart, mind and body are at optimum. When not coherent, function declines. It is probably certain that our biochemistry is linked with our electromagnetic field as it aligns with the frequencies of our organs, respiration, heart rate, blood pressure. Breathing in and out at a five second count is reported to set up coherent resonance frequency between blood pressure, heart rate and respiration. These become coherent with each other and with the Earth's pulse. Negative emotions produce chaotic resonance patterns which cause our mind, heart, and body to become disjointed and fractured from each other and from the rhythm of the Earth.

We can sense emotional fields from a distance, at least around the diameter of our personal space. But, perhaps, sometimes even further, such as when we walk into a room and can feel the quality of energy. We have a saying, "You could have cut the tension with a knife". Many people love the pulse of a crowd which can be energizing, electrifying, inspiring as well as terrifying, destructive, and mindless as a tsunami when it controls a raging mob.

Many animals can sense magnetic fields. It now appears humans have this capacity as well, perhaps greatly diminished by modern living from its vividness for our distant ancestors. Can some of us sense the fields of those around us? Those fields would carry information about the state of the person generating it. What happens when our electromagnetic fields merge and blend in close proximity?

Having experienced the influence of other people on my emotional state, I can personally verify the reality of transmission of information radiating from them and changing my body-heart-mind state in response. When in proximity of a loved one, the encounter releases oxytocin, the so-called "love hormone". When in proximity of a problematic person, I am likely to feel the release of adrenaline and other stress hormones. Sometimes, I know what the other person is going to say before they do so.

Many believe that conscious awareness originates in the brain alone. Recent scientific research suggests that consciousness may emerge from the brain and body acting together. A growing body of evidence suggests that the heart plays a particularly significant role in this process. Shared

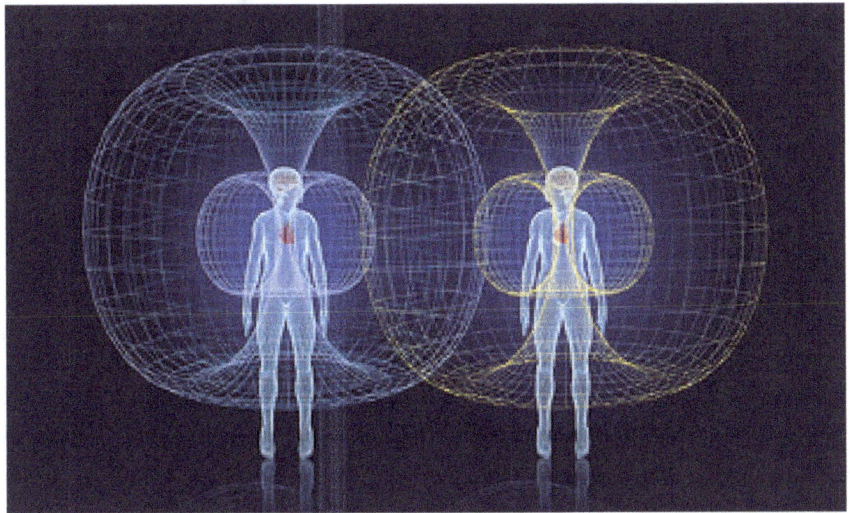

Image 6. "Two Hearts, Two Souls?

feelings, resonating in each other, build new neuronal pathways and strengthen existing ones which leave a change in the architecture of our brain. When we resonate together, this principle suggests that aspects of our brain structure and functioning begin to coincide and, perhaps, mirror each other.

Mirror Neurons

The recent discovery of *"mirror neurons"* suggests that "resonance" is not a metaphor. These specialized neurons, spread throughout my brain, literally function like mirrors. When they "see" behavior, movement, or emotion in others, they fire in the area of my brain that resonates with that activity or feeling. When they fire, they stimulate in my brain, hormones that produce the same type of experience they are recording in the person outside of me. Perhaps we may discover that people recognized as empathic are rich in mirror neurons and those deficient appear insensitive to others, perhaps because, literally, they *do not experience, in themselves*, the pain or joy their eyes are seeing displayed by people in front of them. This may be the basis of sociopathy and autism and other profound relationship disturbances. Research suggests that mirror neurons allow us to guess what other people are thinking. When they trigger my mirrored feeling, my mind starts to think what it would normally think when experiencing these feelings in my body. These research findings suggest that the images we see in night dreams and daydreams, images that can produce strong emotional reactions and sometimes carry profound information, are facilitated by our mirror neurons looking at, and responding to, the images forming in our minds. Mirror neurons seems to turn our brain into a biological virtual reality machine. These mirror neurons link our emotions and thoughts together.

They may also be involved in my awareness of myself, in self-reflection, in listening to inner talking and the extreme experience of feeling *outside* oneself. Why would Nature have developed a way to re-arrange atoms and molecules into such specialized receiving instruments unless to link hearts and minds together ... and perhaps to allow us to escape from the illusion that we are the personality we perceive when we become "self-conscious" (in both senses of the word) and can observe our ordinary self in action in its life? It seems that relationship, shared feelings, and experiences, both with others ... and with *myself* ... is embedded into Nature's design.

Since emotional states are not physical structures, such as material bodies, but rather represent subjective awareness of changes in hormonal and electrical activity in the brain and nervous system, their origin appears to lie in the interactions between molecules, atoms, and electromagnetic fields. This places them in the quantum realm, the dimension where Newtonian laws of the physical universe do not apply. It is the dimension of energy creation and transformation that lies at the heart of the Universe. In this realm, "particles" can become "entangled" with each other and theoretically at long distances. What happens to one is immediately reflected in the other. Some researchers, noticing this similarity, have coined the term, "Quantum Love".

"The experience of falling in love is altogether reminiscent of what, in quantum physics, is known as entanglement. In the microscopic realm, once two particles experience a shared state, they are no longer separate entities but exist as one. This remains true even when they are separated by a great distance. Quantum Love is a term borrowed from quantum physics, the science of how energy works. ... a state where you and your partner are in energetic harmony together in your optimal energetic state, as a couple and individually." *

Of course, every stick has two ends. We also become entangled in negative relationships, like a fly in the spider's web. Not only do countless

---

* *Psychology Today, March 9, 2016*

personal relationships become entrapped in such magnetic whirlpools, but so do communities, religions, nations. The dimension of emotions is, potentially endless. What can help us navigate is being able to distinguish between the experiential feeling of a harmonic, coherent and a non-harmonic, incoherent state of mind, heart, and body. Like the child's game of "hot and cold" ("You're getting warmer ... warmer ... no, now you're getting colder .... Warmer again ... keep going .... now you're hot"), we can learn to follow the compass of our energy.

The Spirituality of Love

Now, at the conclusion of this exploration, I am reflecting back on the painful experience of emptiness when my wife died. Our atmospheres, our fields, had been interpenetrating each other for twenty years. Not only did we share resonance through physical intimacy, but we had engaged in mental and emotional intercourse, impregnating each other with our world views, our values, our shared experiences. That blending had energized and changed us both. We each carried imprints of the other inside ourselves. I had felt her moods, her tensions, her joys, her fears, her wishes, our shared values, and where we conflicted ... all in my interior. I wasn't alone in myself because part of her was inside me. When she left her body, she took her field with her. Its withdrawal from my subjective inner world was experienced as a sudden void. The emptiness was real.

Relationships feed, for better or worse, on each other's shared energy, mutually stimulating the electrical rhythms and biochemical patterns in each person. Physically, emotionally, and mentally, her energy had resonated within me for two decades. Now the source of that radiating emanation was gone. The energy no longer entered and vibrated in me. I felt its absence keenly. The memory of it was a pale facsimile.

When there is a shared resonance in head, heart, and body between people, that quality of harmonic relationship appears to literally represent a joining of Heaven and Earth through the lightning-rod of a human being.

> *From every human being*
> *there rises a light*
> *that reaches straight to heaven.*
> *And when two souls*
> *that are destined to be together*
> *find each other,*
> *their streams of light flow together,*

As Inside, So Outside; As Above, So Below

and a single brighter light goes forth
from their united being.

Two Souls, Baal Shem Tov

Quotations

"If you want to find the secrets of the Universe, think in terms of energy, frequency, and vibration."

Nikola Tesla

"I would rather have questions that can't be answered than questions that can't be asked."

Richard Feynman

The day science begins to study non-physical phenomena, it will make more progress in one decade than in all the previous centuries of its existence.

Nikola Tesla

As Inside, So Outside; As Above, So Below

Being In The World, But Not Of It

O ur culture's historic spiritual heritage has transmitted the recommendation to "be in the world but not of it". What does this mean? This has often been interpreted to mean either physically withdrawing from the world or our responsibility to it. This literal translation seems opposite to the demand to be helpful and responsible in our relationship to people and the world around us, to practice the Golden Rule and to learn to "love everything that breathes"*.†

My experience with Gurdjieff's system of transformation has shown me a different and practical way of understanding this seemingly perplexing recommendation. When trying to enact this saying, I discovered that the illuminating questions are, what do I identify as the "World'? And what do I identify as my "Self?"

I normally live in two worlds, the one outside, with its values and demands, and the one *inside* my heart and mind with *its* conscience and exigencies. What do I do when the values and demands of each are not in accord? In that case, which "world" I give my allegiance to depends on where I locate the abode of 'my' dwelling ... inside my feelings and mind ... or ... outside in the material world of the outer senses and social demands and expectations? When the two conflict, which of these "Masters" do I serve?

After a period of working under Gurdjieff's instructions, as I understood them, I began to notice at least two different levels of motivation and belief inside myself. The values and wishes of "my interior spiritual work felt to be of a higher quality than the wishes and values of my personality and its need for approval, and the safety/comfort concerns of my body and self-image. Which then do I believe is more 'real', in the sense of being closer to my real Self?

Thus, three levels emerge:

---

* Gurdjieff describes this as the "Eighteenth Commandment of Endlessness"
† Beelzebub's Tales to His Grandson, Dutton, NY, 1950, p 198

1. the physical world shown me by my outward focused sense organs.

2. the inner psychological level that is concerned with the safety and comfort of my body and what people think about me, my self-image.

3. and the interior level that is interested in deeper spiritual, inner Work and the potential of freedom from the concerns of my ego. All three of these 'worlds' or levels have their own reality.

The third level that is interested in freedom from my conditioned nature represents a *third world*. From this impartial location we can find a way between yes and no, either-or, black or white.

To this question must be added another historic cultural admonition that "No one can serve two masters, for either he will hate the one and love the other; or else he will be devoted to one and despise the other."*

If I am awake enough in a moment to see the choice, I must choose which to obey in that moment, since I only have that moment in which to work. We have to choose which one we will try to follow while, simultaneously, recognizing that other choices exist and have legitimate responsibilities to be met at their own level.

One way Gurdjieff explores these responsibilities is by introducing five sacred strivings into his story of mankind's fall and possible redemption. We are to strive to become responsible for the appropriate maintenance of our bodies and the awakening and perfecting of Conscience first... so that we may then acquire the ableness to participate in "lightening the burden" of the World ... and its Creator ... by assisting others in moving towards their own individual perfection. These four strivings bracket the connecting recommendation that we also consciously strive to know "the laws of world creation and world maintenance" ... that we must have practical understanding of how things actually work so that we don't get lost in useless fantasy. The five strivings are not an "either-or" option. Each one rests upon the one before, so that the final integration is like a Russian nesting doll.

The New Testament gives another suggestion for balancing this formula: "Render unto Caesar what is Caesar's and unto God that which belongs to God". Its teaching also eliminates "either-or" by telling us to "Love *God* and your neighbor *as* yourself".

---

* *Matthew 6:24*

Using Gurdjieff's terminology, it is a question of *identification*. Can I fulfill my responsibilities, financial, interpersonal, to the legitimate well-being of my body and those around me, without placing these practical necessities on the altar of my inner worship? Have I made the life of my body and personality my inner god instead of seeing them as part of my stewardship to the 'world' outside my inner awareness?

It is possible to serve the material world of the senses and the ordinary psychological world of people, including my ordinary myself, ... as a servant of the Work,* or God, or Endlessness, or Atman or my highest values ... and not to gain anything for my ego out in the world. This can happen when in a state that allows me the *experience of being a Witness* to the manifestations of my personality, and *its* belief that *it* is the acme of Consciousness ... without believing that this personality pattern represents my highest potential.

Another recommendation for practice to become available to this more objective state is that one must "pray in private" and not outwardly to show off to others one's piety. We are told not to seek reward or recognition from the world outside, but rather to pray for peace in "heaven", the "kingdom", two names for a higher state of consciousness said to reside within us but rarely visited.

It is my repeated experience over many years, that when intentionally "sensing" my physical body, the perception of "myself" as something *inside* the body begins to appear. This experience confirms that I have a body, I am surrounded by a body, but I, myself, am *something which becomes differentially aware inside my body*, while my physical, material form itself is now experienced as an object out in the 'world' immediately surrounding ... but *outside* my interior psychological space.

One difficulty arises when I believe I am my body. Then my ego, my *assumed* 'true' self, identifies itself with the body and the material world the body must live in. From this limited perspective I experience myself as part of the world outside and do not realize that I am actually a *mysterious something experiencing itself from inside a surrounding body*. If I can experience myself within my physicality as my body deals with the physical world, then I would realize that "I" am a witness to it, but "not of it".

---

* "The Work": one name for Gurdjieff's complex, multi-leveled system of transformation. It also represents the Perrennial Wisdom passed down through the ages, a modern version of which is Gurdjieff's "Work" or "Fourth Way"

When I believe that my personality and *I* are the same thing, my psychic functions are then dedicated to their image and comfort in the outside world. I get confused by the question of how to be in the world but not of it and think I must literally 'give it all away' … leave the world and renounce earthly desires. Rather, what I must give up is my identification of *Myself* as located in personality.

When I can begin to feel *my Self* located deeper … higher … in the direction of That Which Sees and silently witnesses without judgment, then the apparent paradox disappears. Being in the world but not of it is not a question of how, but more a question of *Being*.

When "I Am", I have the experience and understand the deeper truth.

Time-Body

O n a warm summer's evening, as night falls and fireflies dance in the darkening field, the children are playing with celebratory sparklers. What I have always enjoyed most about these small, hand-held fireworks, is watching the visible lines traced in the air when waving them in circles and figure eights. Since the point of light is moving more rapidly than our eyes can habituate to its bright glow, we see the tracing of where the light had been in its arc and swirl around the body of the celebrant waving it through the air. Because our eyes continue to react to where the light had been as well as where it is in the moment, we can literally see the trace of its life in time, written on our retina but projected out into the space in front of us. What we are seeing is the "Time Body" of the sparkler's brief existence, the line its life traveled from birth to death.

Image 7. Star (sparkler) from Pixabay.com

Most phenomena move either too fast or too slow for us to have a sensory impression of the shape of their existence in space and time.

As Above

Looking up at the planets and stars, beginning to appear in the darkening sky I realize, through my mind's ability to visualize and conceptualize, that I am seeing only the briefest moment in the millions or billions of Earth years comprising the lifetime of those celestial bodies. The Earth's rotation is too slow to allow me to easily see the stars and planets actually moving along their "path" across Earth's sky. Over a matter of minutes, I can see that stars near the horizon seem to have "risen" higher in the heavens. Understanding that this is an illusion and that my vision is being carried by the Earth's movement in relation to the "fixed" star, I can "trace" the invisible arc of the rising points of light by consulting my memory of their position several

Image 8. Stars, Imgur.com

minutes in the "past". I intuit movement more than actually experience it. Time-lapse photography extends our visual sense and does allow us to see the imprint of the illusion of moving stars in the night sky. A multi-hour exposure would allow us to see a multi-hour slice of the time-body of the stars as viewed from Earth.

The stars themselves have their own motion relative to their neighbors and to the galactic center itself. Most stars are binaries, they have twins. Some have more than one companion and some are solitary, like our Sun appears to be, although there is speculation about a theoretical twin hiding in plain sight among thousands of objects encircling the solar system. Computer generated projections of these movements over time show a very different picture than our limited eyes can reveal. Like a child's sparkler, swirling lines denote the path taken through space by each light source as it moves under the influence of the cumulative gravitational fields in which it is embedded.

When viewing a galaxy, including our own Milky Way, the vast majority of stars are not individually visible. Their collective light blends together to produce an image more resonant with the Time-Body of the galaxy than that of its constituent suns. This gives galaxies a "shape" perceptible to our eyes. That apparent shape changes when viewed in non-visible wavelengths which disclose structure not accessible to the visible light spectrum which our eyes depend up to "show us reality."

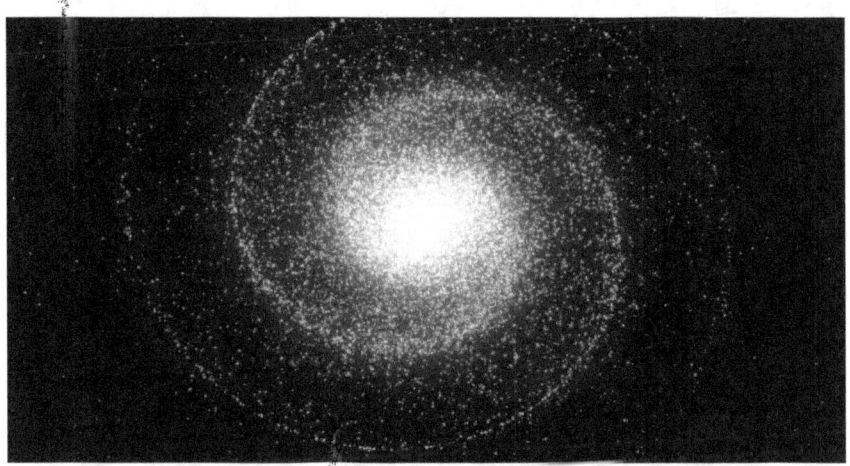

Image 9. Spiral galaxy (Wallpaper Cave)

Galaxies live in neighborhoods, in "galactic clusters". NASA tells us that our cluster is a "relatively small" fifty galaxies while others range up to a thousand or more. Clusters then organize themselves into "superclusters" of up to one hundred thousand. By plotting the direction of their movements in relation with other clusters, computers can trace where they have been and the direction of their travel over deep time. Like the sparklers, a slice of their Time-Body reveals forms that lie far beyond the lifespan of our personal planetary-based timeframe, even beyond the Time-Body of the Earth, and even the life span of our Sun. On the next page (Image 10) is an image of the Time-Body of our supercluster, called Laniakea, holding an estimated 100,000 galaxies. Clusters may span hundreds of millions to billions of light years across.

Closer to home, we can trace the Time-Bodies of the planets as they orbit the sun. The traditional diagram of the solar system is a conceptualized rendering of the path planets take as they move along their

Image10. Computer generated image the location of our galaxy in our galactic super cluster

Image 11. Solar System and Planets

gravitational slot around their star. Like the sparkler, we can then see the lines traced through space giving the impression of the Sun having circles, or rings, around it, like Saturn has rings around its circumference.

This picture (Image 11) is misleading as it is a two-dimensional representation as if the Sun itself were stationary. In this view, the shape of the solar system Time-Body appears spherical. But the Sun is moving along its own orbit around the galactic center, pulling its planets along with it, creating a spiral instead of the circle seen from a top-down viewing."

But the Sun's trajectory is not flat. It swims alternately above and below the galactic plane in periods of tens of millions of years as it makes it 250,000,000-year orbit around the galactic center.

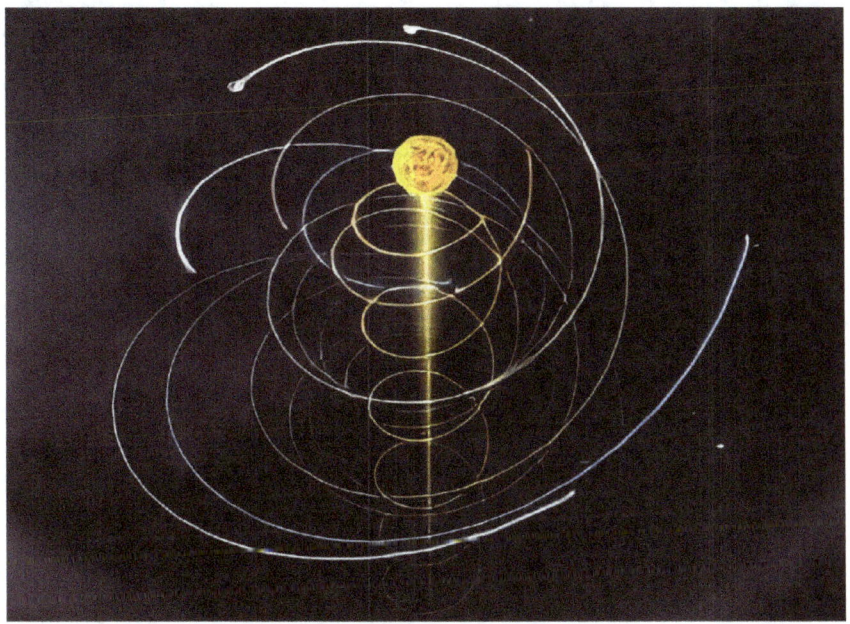

Image 12. The Long Body of the Solar System

If we want to try to understand what a planet or a star or a galaxy or a galactic cluster may actually be, we need to see the shape, the "body" as it appears spread out along the line of its existence (see Images 12, 13 and 14). The lifetimes of these celestial structures infinitely exceed our own. From their point of view, our existence would be a flicker of such miniscule duration as to not "exist" for them from their perspective. In the same way, many of the biological functions of our own physical body happen so rapidly as to be non-perceptible to our senses. Without special instruments we would never know of their existence as their time-body, relative to ours, is less than a flicker. Yet, at the level of their existence, they have all the time they need to perform their function. If they were conscious, our time-body, relative to their own, would move so slowly they could have no sense of our shape or life.

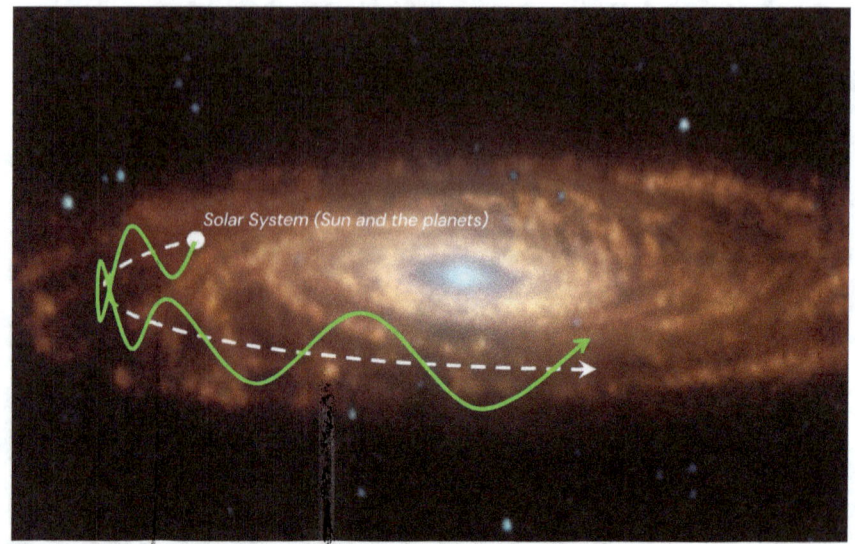

Image 13. The Path of the Solar System Through The Galaxy

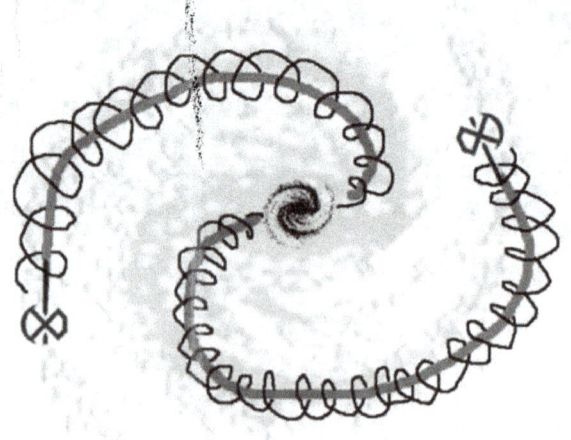

Image 14. The Time Body of a Solar System (DjSadhu)
See https://www.youtube.com/watch?=BiH/sa36_NTU DjSadhu

So Below

This may all be interesting from a philosophical perspective, but there is a critical, practical application. What is the shape of my time-body if viewed from outside my current moment?

The moment I am living is too brief to have much of a shape. The particular event, I am experiencing may have activity, an emotional tone and an intent ... but how does it fit into the pattern of my life? Which part of the puzzle is this instance? What can it tell me, or anyone else, about who I am, where I have been, what I have experienced, what I have learned, what type of person I am?

When we examine our personal history, as best we understand it, we splice together a story from the fragments we can remember. I was born here, and then went to school there and met so-and-so and did such-and-such ... and now I am here. Tomorrow I will be in a different moment. Eventually I will run out of moments and die. Then, I *presume*, my timeline stops.

A primitive way of exploring this would be to trace, on a map, all the places you have traveled over the span of your years. This would represent a crude time-body line of your physical movements during your life to date. If you were able to draw in such a way that the 1,000 trips to grandma's house would be etched deeper and darker on the map than the solo trip to Tahiti, this would begin to provide a little more dimensionality. You could also add your accomplishments, successes, and failures, to get a taste of your social time-body as viewed by those around you.

You might, perhaps, also try to color-code movements or areas of strong emotional experience, places in the timeline that really affected you. This adds a beginning exploration of the internal time-body which always accompanies the physical body as it moves through its life activities on the surface of Earth. This is the subjective psychological world of thought, feeling, imagination, creative speculation, and theorizing. It is the world in which we carry our understanding, our hurts and grievances, our self-image, our dreams and wishes. Where has my mind traveled in this higher dimensional realm knowable only to myself?

The life of my physical body is limited to the physical world. The life of my psychological body is not limited by space nor time, nor reality. Yet all these inner experiences mark the quality of my Being and the capacity of my level of consciousness and, thus, has a strong influence on the form of my visible life outside, including the activities and health of my material body. This subjective dimension is real and is the dominant factor in most of the manifestations of people. To not become familiar with it, is to leave myself blind and helpless in the grip of mindless, conditioned habits and patterns. Is my interior, subjective time-body, only my own business? As it affects all those around me, it is certainly not isolated to myself alone. I am being irresponsible to myself and the world around me if I do not accurately understand where I am at a given moment in my inner world ... in what part, with what attitude, with which catalogue of selective memories, and at what level of maturity?

The question which haunts self-aware life, is the question of whether anything of this subjective interior world survives the death of the body. It is difficult to impossible to ponder this from only the perspective of the material aspect of the entire time-body. But ... since the higher part of the time-body, the part invisible to all except oneself, is not of the material world, perhaps the rules of physical nature do not apply in that location.

My past lives within me, even though the body I occupied at the time memories were encoded no longer exists in the form it took years ago. The future speculations I make in imagination when I visit a potential time that might come, do not have a material existence. They reside in my mind and heart. Attempts to understand this higher dimensional existence are turning to the apparent quantum nature of subjective awareness. The quantum realm underlies the physical and operates according to very different laws. In this realm, something can be in two places at the same time. Two somethings far apart can become "entangled" and communicate with each other instantaneously. Electrons can jump from one orbit around a nucleus to another orbit without traversing the space in between.

In my subjective world, events spaced many years apart can be related and mutually influencing. I can be in two places at once as when I "am of two minds". My attention can jump from one topic to another without apparent connection. If my subjective awareness, the capacity that makes me aware of my existence, is a quantum phenomenon ... then I am ... my consciousness is ... a quantum phenomenon.

As I can confirm that my subjective awareness has a time-body life beyond the senses of the corporeal body, then perhaps the experiences of my psychological time-body may be less dependent on my material existence than I supposed. And, if it is a citizen of the quantum dimension underlying and interpenetrating the physical world of Space-Time, then it would share that world with all other subjective awareness in a blending of shared awareness in a higher world. That blended awareness would have its own, perhaps, eternal time-body.

The Body of Humankind

I magine back in time to the appearance of our homo sapiens ancestors. In the beginning there were very, very few of these early humans. Let's say, as an analogy for this exploration that, in the beginning, two of the first men and women mated and produced two children. Now there are four. The children found mates and had each had two children. Now there are ten. Then the four children found mates and produced ...

Multiply this progression out over perhaps two or three hundred thousand years. Today there are nearly eight billion descendants of this metaphorical couple. Visualize this enormous pyramid reaching from an eight-billion-pixel base to a razor sharp, pixel point at the top.

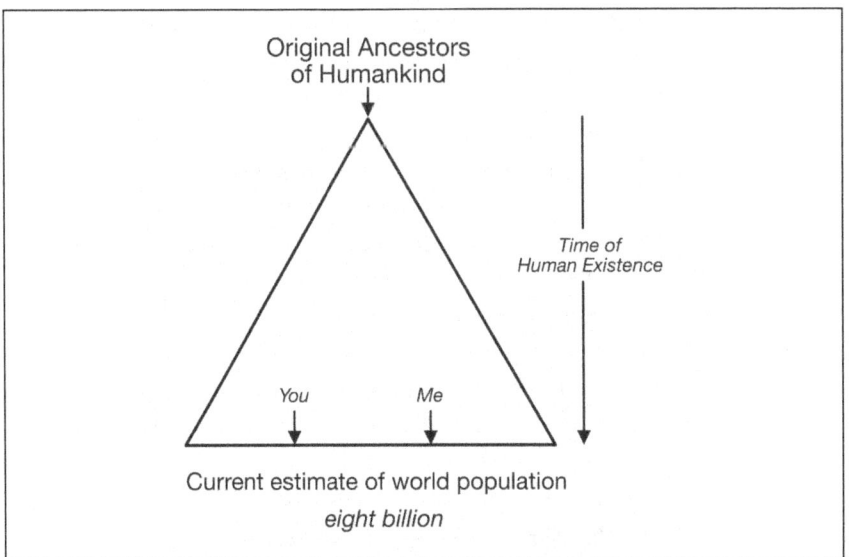

Figure 1. The Population Pyramid

Now imagine one these nearly eight billion people. Imagine yourself. You are a single point, a single pixel. You had two parents. Your two

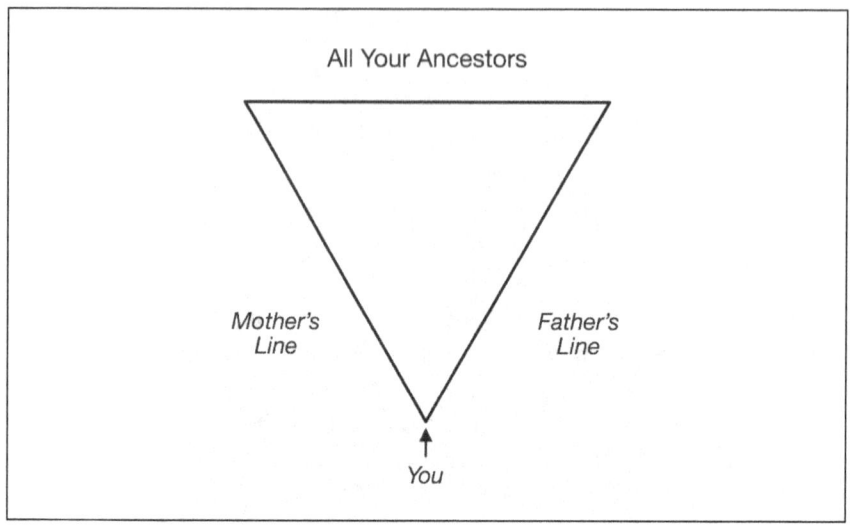

Figure 2. The Inverted Pyramid

parents had four parents between them. Those four parents had eight parents and those eight had sixteen and ...

All the people above you, further back in time, all your ancestors, have ancestors above them and their ancestors have ancestors above them and ...

Now, you are the inverted apex of an enormous pyramid of personal genetic contributors reaching back to an integrated mass of nearly all the people who have every lived ... all are your ancestors. Even more strangely, every one of the eight billion of us is also the apex of the triangle, as at some point all the individually initiated triangles overlap. All of us are the descendants of these two hypothetical members of the original tiny group of new humans who began the process.

If we look at the block of time humans have been on Earth as a solid, continuous presence, we can overlap both triangles to represent the span of human existence.

What emerges is an ancient symbol (see next page). In our Western heritage known as the Star of David or the Seal of Solomon, it is the symbol of the Jewish Nation from antiquity. It represents, in this exploration, the inter-connectedness of our species as a "solid" something, that constitutes the time frame of human existence on the planet. It is in this way that one could sense the concept of a timeless Universal

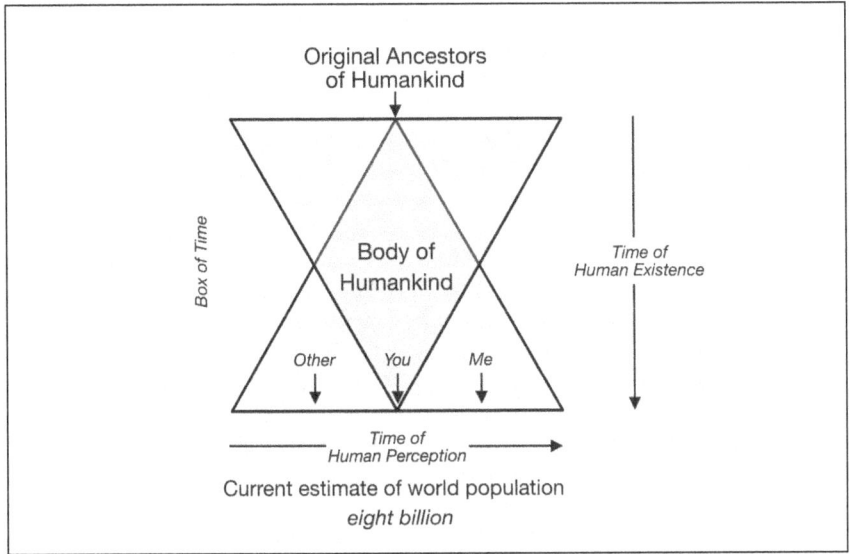

Figure 3. The Star of David

Humankind in which each of us is a cell in the accumulating and expanding body of this unique lifeform. To see an outline of this Body of the Species, we can look to the mystery of the blended triangles. They appear opposite, one inverted and the other upright. Yet they are also the same, two sides of the same "something", *the higher dimensional* Body of Humankind existing outside of our brief, personal time frame. To us, as short-lived individuals, it would seem *immortal*. From the perspective of the Earth, it is a blink of the planetary eye.

As every cell in a body has both an individual life and a role to play in the maintenance and health of the larger whole to which it belongs, so too do we, individual 'cells' though we may be, have a role to play in the unimaginably huge and ancient Body of Humankind ... which, itself, has a role to play in the time body of the Earth ... perhaps as the Earth may have a role to play in the body of the solar system ... perhaps as the solar system may have a role to play in the galaxy ... as the galaxy may have a role to play in the Universe.

Somewhere in all this infinite complexity, there is a role for Humankind. And deeper still, inside the body of humankind, there is a role for each of us individuals in the infinitely brief moment of our existence on this planet.

As Inside, So Outside; As Above, So Below

A Thin Sensitive Film

I recall vividly the moment of shock I experienced on first reading P. D. Ouspensky's *In Search of the Miraculous,* the thrill of electricity running through my body, and the stunned feeling of a huge reality looming above me like a tidal wave. Ouspensky referred to life as a *thin sensitive film* clinging to the surface of the planet. Of course, I knew this was factually true, but "knowing" it from my intellectual collection of information did not prepare me for the actual *feeling of the reality* of it. In that moment I saw an image of the Earth surrounded by its atmosphere and a less than razor thin 'film' of animal and plant life smeared on the surface.

Today I was driving along a rural road near my home in Maine. I was aware of the scenery, the occasional car approaching, my body controlling the vehicle ... and simultaneously ... I was aware of thoughts and images in my mind. I was pondering the juxtaposition of these two dimensions, the material world of mass-based bodies and my mental-emotional and sensory world of subjective experiences inside.

The radio was on. A man was talking about international tensions and the violent repercussions that might ensue from the belief systems and egoist motivations of powerful leaders. I saw how these events threatening the stability of the world outside, were the direct result of inner events in the psyche of only a few "power possessors" who were about to wreak havoc on the lives of hundreds of thousands to satisfy the fantasied vainglory of their imagination of themselves.

At the same time, I saw that the less dramatic events in the lives of myself and those about me, were also projected manifestations from the subjective psychological world inside of us all. Our subjective world is embedded *within* the thin film of life ... and influencing it from this interior location.

Then I saw something else. The surrounding trees in this area stood about 30 feet tall. Above them was the sky and above the sky was outer space and the entire Universe all the way to its end ... if it has an end.

I looked at the cars on the road carrying their human operators. Then I saw the people in the cars. Most of us, when standing, were on average between five and six feet from the surface of the Earth. I saw that there was nothing between the tops of our heads and the end of the Universe either.

Then I experienced myself as something like the tiniest of crawling insects, stuck to the surface of our planet, living out my entire life, except when temporarily on an airplane, with my head only a few feet from the surface. I am part of that razor-thin smear of organic goo.

This organic film was continually processing food, liquid, atmospheric gases ... and photons from the sun ... transforming them into higher qualities of energy by taking apart their molecular and atomic components, reconstructing them into different patterns and, in the process, bringing into itself, from its environment, sources of energy to transform into life, sensitivity and subjective awareness. The film was alive and an energy transformer. The individual life forms within the film were like cells in its 'body'.

This is what I am. I am an infinitesimal living biological dot, an organelle within a razor-thin planetary film, stuck to a large, round rock floating in an infinite space with no dimensions and no time. I perceive myself as "right side up", feet on the ground head pointing up. But I am on a ball. Therefore, simultaneously, I am also sticking out sideways from the surface. I am also upside down with my feet stuck to the ceiling and my head pointing down ... and out ... towards the stars. It is a matter of perspective.

When I now imagine myself on the "bottom" of the giant ball, I feel a little queasy, seeing myself hanging 'upside down'. If gravity vanished, I would fall down and away from the Earth, head-first with my feet up "above" me. If I see myself on the 'top', I would lift off the ground and float upward. Both views are true.

What are the implications of this fact? What does this mean ... a universe with no down or up, no west or east, no south or north ... just suspended in a void, held as an eternal captive in the embrace of a star?

And my body is less than a pinprick on the surface, imperceptible ... unless viewed from its own level. From my location, the surface around me seems flat, huge, solid, immobile. In truth, it is curved and eternally in motion at implausible speeds, spinning on its axis, orbiting its star, circling its galaxy, and traveling with a neighborhood of other galaxies along an invisible river of countless galactic communities, all flowing towards infinity.

From my perspective, the world of my life is lived within a few feet of the Earth's surface. As I drive through the forest, I think again of ants moving through their equivalent forest of grass. That is their world, down at my feet. They can know nothing of the higher world above them ... nor I of the higher worlds above me..

From the larger perspective, the low ceiling of my world almost makes me a citizen of "Flatland". Because of my tiny size, I don't feel claustrophobic. I avoid this sense of disproportion because my conditioned thinking is shaped by what my senses show me and by the stories, and interpretations I make inside my psychological world. To see the larger picture, I must go into my mind and construct images to match this higher understanding.

Image 8. The Earth from Saturn (NASA)

My psychological world seems to accompany my brain, so it too is located a fraction from the surface of the planet. But, on the other hand, my imagination is not tied to the surface. It is not bound by time. It can travel into future and past. It can take itself into imaginary worlds. It can create an image for itself so that it is looking back on Earth from the rings of Saturn. The mind does not appear to be only part of the living smear on the surface.

And this is my situation. It is your situation too, dear Reader. You can't make this stuff up and yet it is true. If we take time to not only think about this, but *experience the feel of its reality* ... what in the world ... or ... out of the world ... is this all about? As I am part of this ... what does this imply about the mystery of myself?

Cosmology and Consciousness:
Ancient and Contemporary

Since before recorded history, humankind has sought for relationship with ... and/or ... understanding of ... the forces of Nature and the mystery of Life. Initially, and until the last few centuries, the search was predominantly for relationship ... how to communicate with, implore, beseech, thank, or worship, the *Ineffable Mystery* felt to lie behind the observable life in which we are all embedded. Earlier approaches could only be metaphorical and poetic... all based on the *visions, intuitions*, and *experiences* of their founders long in the past.

The great mystery of existence, as is still the case today, was correctly ascribed to invisible forces and energies. Unlike the non-anthropomorphizing scientific approach today, these invisible forces were accepted as highly intelligent, and also, emotionally unpredictable ... like humans ... and then personified and given names. This allowed for the possibility of developing a relationship and thus favor with these forces.

Some of our modern understandings about the origins of the Universe and its underlying atomic structure were already reflected in ancient religious beliefs and philosophy. The Vedas, ancient sacred texts of Hinduism, contain hymns and verses that explore the nature and origins of existence ... the idea of creation emerging from a state of non-existence or cosmic void.

> *"Then even nothingness was not, nor existence.*
>
> *There was no air then, nor the heavens beyond it.*
>
> *What covered it?*
>
> *Where was it?*
>
> *In whose keeping?*
>
> *Was there then cosmic water, in depths unfathomed?*
>
> *Then there was neither death nor immortality nor was there*

then the torch of night and day.

The One breathed windlessly and self-sustaining.

There was that One then, and there was no other." *

The imagery of Vishnu opening and closing his eyes symbolizes the cyclical process of creation and dissolution, suggesting that the universe comes into existence when Vishnu "awakens" and ceases to exist when he "withdraws."

A summary of modern interpretations of this phrasing has been translated as,

"Brahma sleeps in the cosmic ocean, and the lotus of the universe grows from his navel. On the lotus sits Brahma, the creator. Brahma opens his eyes, and a world comes into being, governed by an Indra. Brahma closes his eyes, and a world goes out of being. The life of a Brahma is 432,000 years. When he dies, the lotus goes back, and another lotus is formed, and another Brahma."

This translation concludes:

"Then think of the galaxies beyond galaxies in infinite space, each a lotus, with a Brahma sitting on it, opening his eyes, closing his eyes".

The Hebrew description in Genesis states:

"In the beginning God created the heavens and the earth. Now the earth was formless and empty, darkness was over the surface of the deep, and the Spirit of God was hovering over the waters. And God said, 'Let there be light,' and there was light."†

Current Cosmology

Interestingly, current cosmological thought has also formulated the "Big Bang" theory to describe a Universe that seems to have appeared from nowhere ... theoretically an infinitely tiny, infinitely dense, point given the mysterious name, "Singularity" ... another version of: "All was darkness and then there was light" ... reflecting Genesis and the Rigveda. A version of the Big Bang story says that the Universe may reach a maximum expansion and then contract into a Big Crunch, only to expand again in an endless cycle ... like the cycles of Vishnu.

The Big Bang theory is now being complexified by the "Multiple Universe" theory which speculates that there are an infinite number of Uni-

---

* Nasadiya Sukta (Creation Hymn) found in the Rigveda.
† Genesis 1:1-3 (NIV)

verses and that when they bump each other a new Universe appears ... a commonality with the repeating Universes suggested by Hinduism. Unfortunately, this version just kicks the can down the road by explaining the origin of our Universe without explaining how the first Universe which created all the others came into existence.

In addition, the phrase "Multiverse" is an oxymoron as the term "Uni" denotes one. There can only be one Universe no matter how extensive or how many seemingly separate components it contains. If what we recognize as "our Universe" it is part of something larger, then this simply means the Universe is much larger and complex than originally theorized.

The ancient ideas of *panspermia* ... that the Universe is alive ... and *panpsychism* ... that the Universe is conscious ... appeared in Western literature at least twenty-five centuries ago in ancient Greece. It is a fundamental tenet of Gurdjieff's cosmology as well as having a reflection today in Buddhism and a number of new-age spiritual movements. Largely dismissed by modern science as poetic superstition, a host of recent scientific discoveries have revived interest in these ancient intuitive perspectives. Science has recently discovered:

1. **Organic Molecules** – Complex organic molecules in interstellar space suggesting that the building blocks of life may be widespread throughout the universe.

2. **Extremophiles** – organisms capable of surviving in extreme environments on Earth, which suggests that life may be more resilient and adaptable than previously thought, potentially increasing the likelihood of survival during interplanetary transfer.

3. **Meteorites Containing Organic Compounds,** necessary ingredients for life could have been delivered to Earth via meteorite impacts.

4. **Microbial Survivability in Space:** certain microorganisms can survive and even thrive in the harsh conditions of outer space, including exposure to vacuum, radiation, and extreme temperatures. This raises the possibility that microbial life could survive long journeys through space.

5. **Planetary Exchange:** evidence of meteorite impacts containing microbial life from one planet to the other.

In the search for the origins of conscious awareness, current research and theorizing in fields as diverse as Integrated Information Theory and Quantum Mechanics, has led to renewed interest in panpsychism. IIT suggests that any sufficiently integrated system could possess some form of consciousness, including simple systems like networks of neurons or even fundamental particles. Some Quantum Mechanics interpretations imply that consciousness plays a fundamental role in the collapse of the quantum wave function implying that consciousness is not just an emergent property of complex brains but may be inherent in the fabric of reality itself.

A New Theory

The Electric Universe theory challenges the current Standard Cosmological model and suggests that it is the interaction between electro-magnetic fields acting on plasma ... and not gravity and nuclear fusion ... fusion ... that provides the primary power that drives and shapes the Universe. The discovery of rivers of electro-magnetic currents flowing through and between celestial bodies throughout the Universe has led some researchers to speculate that, rather than the slow effects of gravity pulling clouds of interstellar gases into sufficient density to ignite stars through thermonuclear explosion, what causes new stars to ignite and planets to be born, is the pressure from these organized electro-magnetic rivers in the midst of nebulae plasma gases.

Dating back to ancient Greece, *plasma* ... also known, here on Earth, in one of its forms as *fire* ... has been recognized as the fourth fundamental state of matter, along with *earth, water*, and *air* in the ancient language ... *solid, liquid, and gaseous* in our contemporary language. Plasma is a state of matter, where a gas is so energetic that it can conduct electricity and is highly responsive to magnetic fields. Astronomers tell us that it makes up 99.9 % of the matter of the universe, not only between the sun and its planets, but between stars and galaxies. Space, until recently, was assumed to be a total vacuum. Now it is understood to be a universal field of pulsating, electrically charged plasma of infinite potential energy.

Interestingly, experiments have demonstrated that electrical currents in plasma fields can produce complex patterns that are reflective of forms found on prehistoric rock art, ancient symbols and in Mandalas and religious art. The study called "Cymatics", passing vibrations through different materials like sand or water or rice on a resonating surface, can produce an image of the vibrational frequency being transmitted through it, just as iron filings reveal the shape of the magnet's field. These images also can reflect complex forms reminiscent of mandalas and other symbols.

It is as if the form is transmitted, in code, through the vibration into a medium that organizes itself to reflect the image behind the code ... like the science fiction process of teleportation. The similarity with ancient symbolic imagery and resonance with creation myths about war between the gods in the heavens, has led to speculation that the sky above the heads of our ancient ancestors may have produced extraordinary plasma displays due to a different configuration of the planets at that time and introduced the stimulus for the form of mythologies passed down to us today but assumed to be only the product of ancient imaginations. These new theories, regarded by mainstream cosmology as "pseudoscience", may or may not turn out to be better explanations than current understanding, but they are interesting attempts to address the holes in current theory that remain unresolved.

Bioelectricity

Life, our brain, and nervous system, run on *bioelectricity*. Whether electromagnetism is the major or a subsidiary force maintaining and shaping the Universe, the existence of bioelectricity within us would suggest an immediate link and potential blending of our minds and bodies into the universal fabric.

We still do not understand what we are, why anything exists or even what we can actually fathom of the implausible fact of existence. Recent observations from the Webb telescope currently threaten to undermine the Big Bang explanation and send modern cosmology back to the drawing board.

The addition of human reason to the search, beginning as far back as the ancient Greeks, introduced the possibility of bringing the creative intellectual impulse to wonder *how* these unfathomable phenomena, *actually worked*. What were the processes that underlay their expression? Were they predictable or would humankind always be at the mercy of unpredictable gods?

Today, science correctly congratulates itself for discovering a method of investigation through which theories can be verified to an accepted mathematical standard by measuring the probability of the result occurring by chance. Replication of the experiment can provide further confirmation and recognition that the experimental model is useful. Observation, theorizing, testing the theory and observing more, have allowed us to unravel some of the laws that appear to govern how things work in the Universe. But the discovery of how observable processes work is not the same as understanding the meaning of this infinitely complex, multi-dimensional, Universe of which we are a living part.

Conventional scientists ... and many of their devoted followers ... seem to believe that knowing how something works is the same as understanding what it means that the phenomenon exists ... or... that since meaning is irrelevant to, or beyond the purview of, science, it need not be taken into account when trying to understand existence. Science is not equipped to address meaning, but only process. How else then can the deeper mysteries of existence be explored if science is limited to studying the observables ... but not the intangibles?

Inspiration and Conceptualization: The Original Instruments

There are two other ways to relate to this question. In addition to *Physical Cosmology* which studies the forces organizing and maintaining the physical world, i.e. astronomy, astrophysics, physics, biology, mathematics, there is a *Religious Cosmology* in every origin story and a *Metaphysical Cosmology* utilized by philosophers and mystics who explore the Universe through the use of their minds, thought experiments, dreams, and insights.

Thousands of years ago, Vedic texts explored the nature of *light and consciousness*. The Upanishads, for instance, associated light with the inner self and spiritual growth. New theories of consciousness are postulating that subjective awareness is an aspect of the quantum world ... as is light. Dr. Keith Buzzell suggests that *Attention* itself, is photonic in nature.* Sir Roger Penrose, Oxford University mathematical physicist and Nobel Lauriate, hypothesizes that consciousness has quantum origins.

The concept of the atom, as an indivisible fundamental particle that makes up matter, was postulated by ancient Greek philosophers, such as Leucippus and Democritus in the 5th century BCE. Democritus first used

---

* *Buzzell, Keith; A New Conception of God: Further Reflections on Gurdjieff's Whim, 2013, Fifth Press, Salt Lake City, Utah*

the term *"atomos,"* meaning indivisible or uncuttable, to describe these fundamental particles. He proposed that everything in the universe is composed of tiny, indivisible particles called atoms, which differ in size, shape, and arrangement. Democritus envisioned these atoms as in constant motion, combining and recombining to form various substances ... just as we have come to understand through modern science.

Several scientific breakthroughs first appeared in the dreams and intuitions of their discoverers. The shape of the six-carbon atom benzene ring appeared to Augustus Kekule, when he dreamt of a snake eating its tail. A hallmark of Albert Einstein's career was his use of visualized thought-experiments. The concept of relativity appeared to him in a dream. After Niels Bohr dreamt of electrons orbiting their nucleus like a solar system, he went on to win the 1922 Nobel Prize in Physics for discovering the structure of the atom.

Building on these historical facts, and personal experience with altered states of consciousness, in 1973 NASA astronaut Edward Mitchell founded the Institute for Noetic Sciences to study the mystery of consciousness and its reported paranormal manifestations.

Two decades later, in 1994, The Journal of Consciousness Studies began publication as an interdisciplinary peer-reviewed academic journal dedicated to the field of consciousness studies.

The use of psychedelic plants in vision quests dates back thousands of years and is deeply rooted in various indigenous cultures across the world. One of the earliest pieces of evidence of psychedelic plant use can be traced to ancient rock paintings and cave art, which depict scenes possibly related to shamanic rituals and ceremonies involving altered states of consciousness. Similar evidence has been found in other regions, such as the Americas and South Asia, suggesting the long history of using psychoactive substances in spiritual and religious practices. Additionally, archaeological discoveries of artifacts like bowls, pipes, and vessels with residues of psychoactive substances in different parts of the world also provide evidence of early human use of these plants for ritualistic or visionary purposes.

If the current scientific approach to understanding is the only method for discovery, how do we explain the ancient perceptiveness now being confirmed many thousands of years later by contemporary scientists ... the greatest of whom make their own discoveries in the non-mass-based dimension of dream, intuition, imagination, and epiphany? Modern science lays appropriate stress on being "objective" to overcome the long history of suggestibility and superstition. But the observation, study and conclusions drawn by scientists from their sense-enhancing instruments, occur in the subjective, non-material dimension of mind. *It is through the subjective realm of existence, the psychological world of mind, that emerge the ideas to be tested by science. Science is the method. The mind is the discoverer.*

Modern Psychology

Modern psychology, emerging in the late 1800's, and wishing to be a hard science like geology, biology, or physics, likes to stress its "evidence-based" conclusions as being objective. How do the chemical, biological, electrical activities in bodies produce their interactions with life? These engineering questions about the physical body and its neurological phenomena have led to amazing understanding of the mechanics. But the mechanistic viewpoint assumes that the mind is an attribute of the body and not an energy inhabiting a body receptive to its manifestations. It generally doesn't recognize the *relativity of inner experiences*, that although most are *mechanical* and mundane, there are others that display *higher qualities* of originality, unpredictableness, epiphanies … wisdom "beyond one's years" … which change humankind through religious revelation or scientific breakthrough.

But the original and deepest purview of psychology is the *subjective realm of life …* the *direct experiencing of it* and *how that experience is understood.* Its name originates from the Greek term "psyche" which represented the principle of life, breath, and "Soul". In its purest form, psychology can be understood as the study of the Soul.

Recent research has revealed that under some circumstances, the brain begins a response, *fractions of a second* before the person is aware of "making a decision". The recognition of the speed of neurological conditioned responses raises the question, "Do we have Free Will?". The question is framed in black and white … either we have *Free Will* or we don't. It is assumed that if some responses are conditioned and therefore not free, then all responses are conditioned and not free. Not recognized is the possibility of *levels of awareness*, levels of *relative freedom* from some conditioned reactions. If this hierarchical viewpoint is entertained, a different question arises. Under what circumstances do we have more

124

freedom of Will, and under which do we have less?

Contemporary academic psychology abandoned its philosophical roots in the late 19th and early 20th centuries to apply the scientific method to study human behavior and the phenomena of mind through controlled experiments. This has led today to a number of research specialties and clinical applications such as behaviorism, cognitive psychology, neurobiology ... to name a few ... to study mental, behavioral and brain activities. This movement towards a more academic, mechanistic view of the human being has led to great understanding of how the mind-body interface works but has brought us no closer to answering the question of the ghost in the machine which has idiosyncratic experiences, derives a personal sense of meaning from events and channels a creative impulse that often appears in dreams and visions.

The Hard Question of Consciousness

To practically address this most difficult mystery, what is known as the "hard question of consciousness", the field of clinical psychology sought to understand, and then modify, feelings, thought patterns and behaviors. William James, Sigmund Freud and Carl Jung were among the pioneers in postulating and attempting to explore the "unconscious" ... the dark region behind our ordinary awareness ... in which it was hypothesized that disturbances and unhealed trauma lay hidden and influencing the person's feelings and reactions without them being aware of the cause. This invisible region also appeared to be the source of inspiration, fantasy, creativity, and divine revelation.

Those interested in understanding the *nature of mind, its architecture,* and higher potentials, moved in the direction of models of applied psycho-exploration which relied, out of necessity, more on subjective personal reports of inner experiences rather than observing the correlation between externally observable phenomena and underlying mechanical features of the body's chemistry and wiring. The exploration of this strange and largely unknown dimension of subjective experience, led in time to the plethora of *depth psychology* therapeutic approaches available today. All offer degrees of usefulness, but one size does not fit all.

Many therapies prevalent today focus on maladaptive conditioned behaviors with little emphasis on underlying motivation. Others focus on interactive variables like family, social and societal pressures. Others are more concerned with the influence of deeper, more idiosyncratic factors and have a wide range of expression in existential, humanistic, trans-formational approaches which focus on both personal and archetypal *meaning* as factors in psychological functioning. Because the application of these depth approaches, although each having an underlying theory and established methods of exploration, must, to some extent, be individualized to each person, their design is not well suited to traditional materialistic-science research paradigms and are thus not considered "scientific".

Yet, it is these depth approaches that engage the mind in open-ended dialogue which has led to practical understanding of how to help people learn about themselves more objectively ... as well as uncovering, again and again, ancient symbols and themes in dreams and free association which echo the myths and understandings of ancient mystics and philoso-phers. It seems to this author, that this *fact* ... the fact of *similarity be-tween ancient perennial wisdom and modern scientific theories and discoveries...* suggests that intuition and inspiration are a foun-dational part of our exploration of the Universe. *Objective fact is first grasped within the subjective mind.* From the subjective mind emerge concepts and plans to design instruments to validate the ideas against observable, testable variables. It is also an objective fact that the intuitions and inspirations behind the concepts and ideas appear first in the mysterious, subjective mind.

The great difficulty is separating the wheat from the chaff. The sub-jective world contains a mixture of the personal and the transpersonal, accurate interpretations and conditioned misunderstandings, adaptive and maladaptive programmed reactions. What is pure idiosyncratic fantasy and what is, actually, reflective of transpersonal experience.?

During my personal search, I have been aided immeasurably by two transformational approaches to this question. Many years working in Jungian analysis and in G. I. Gurdjieff's Fourth Way system, have helped me to explore this distinction. It has also been both gratifying and con-firming that my research has frequently led me to the words and images of those who have gone before ... only to discover that their words and images were similar or identical to those which had already appeared to me from the depths of my own mind in years prior to discovering that I was only one in a long, long line of predecessors uncovering the same impressions over and over again.

The rapidity of our exponentially expanding scientific understanding is being fueled by a trend towards *interdisciplinary* research. As the space telescopes are dramatically demonstrating, utilizing multiple wavelengths to look at the same object, shows us many different aspects that are invisible if viewed only through one lens. The mystery of consciousness and its relationship to the other phenomena in the Universe cannot be addressed through the exploration of the material world alone … or through the lens of only one or two specialized areas of study … as it appears connected and interactive with so many aspects of the world around and within the body.

The rigidity of reigning paradigms is sustained by an overrepresentation in the given area of study by "experts' whose careers are built on their belief in the superiority of the model they support. The addition of specialists from other traditions to the pursuit of a question can bring additional perspectives which may enlarge or even displace the currently accepted theory. New ideas from outside a specialized field often lack the granular distinctions given importance by experts in the theory and should be rigorously challenged. But they should be engaged in the exploration rather than ignored or ridiculed as is often the case when egoism takes the place of reason.

Consciousness: An Energy Created … or Received and Processed … by the Brain?

Subjective experience certainly seems to alter, or even to disappear, when there is not sufficient energy in the right locations in the brain. Each of us has personally confirmed this when we notice that we no longer have the energy to think or that we are emotionally exhausted and don't feel anything "at the moment" or are physically worn out and have to change activities to regather energy … not to mention the confirming experiences of illness, sleep and anesthesia.

The current assumption that consciousness is produced by the brain is just that … an *assumption* … and an assumption that is running into blank walls as we delve ever deeper into its mystery. *The alternative possibility is that brains are receivers and transmitters of an energy that we label "consciousness".* If consciousness is a universal energy that can manifest in living forms, then it is plausible to speculate that the experience and manifestations of consciousness fluctuate, depending on … the complexity and architecture of different brains … as well as the energy level of the life form from moment to moment … as well as the content of the mind of the life form acquired over its lifetime ... as well as the natural fluctuation of energy waves. This would be a paradigm shift.

It seems too, that science as a *method*, can be applied to both the discoverable mechanisms that underlie the workings of the material world ... and to some limited degree also to test our subjective experiences. This is a very useful brake on imagination and suggestibility. Gurdjieff provides a method to bring a scientific viewpoint to inner work. Unlike other theorists of the "unconscious" or "subconscious" who typically provide interpretations, based on their preferred theoretical assumptions of the meaning of inner images, to their patients or followers, Gurdjieff demands that his practitioners not believe anything they have not *also confirmed through personal experience* ...observe, test, observe. For example, Gurdjieff, amongst other viewpoints, tells us that we are not our bodies. The practices provided by Gurdjieff of sensing the physicality, the vitality of one's surrounding body, can provide a *verifying experience* for this statement. The implications and personal meaning of this experience are left for individuals to work out for themselves in light of an overarching theme that "one is not one's body".

The meaning of the Universe in which we are embedded and the question of a purpose to our existence, require exploration and understanding of our true nature. Is there more than just accepting membership in the body of all life? Life is a process of digesting itself ... the food to power our bodies and brains so that our physical form eventually becomes renewing fertilizer for the Earth. Are we only material for the continuous exchange of energy? These are questions addressed to a multi-layered, multi-dimensional Universe by the mind of a multi-layered, multi-dimensional creature which calls itself Human.

Brain Zaps

I was deep asleep. The experience began with a flash of brilliant light in the pitch blackness of my mind, immediately followed by a loud, concussive explosion which reverberated in my body. I heard my voice moan loudly in distress. In my mind, it was repeatedly asking, "Did you hear that explosion or was it only in my head? Did you hear that explosion or was it only in my head? Did you hear that explosion or was it only in my head?" Then I was aware that my wife, lying next to me in bed, was trying to wake me up. I became alert. Recognizing where I was, I settled down and returned to sleep. I asked her the next morning if she had heard the sound or was it in my head. She, of course, confirmed that she had heard nothing other than my distress before waking me.

A while later, I was looking at news summaries of the previous day. I read that a meteor had fallen in Texas early evening the previous day. There was a bright flash and a loud explosion.

Given the time differential between Texas and my location in Barcelona, the event would have occurred for me around midnight. What was the time of my experience? Neither of us had checked the hour of the nightmare. We only knew it felt like the dead of night.

I recall that on at least two previous occasions in years past, I had seen a bright spark of light in the blackness of my mind as I lay in bed, either asleep or falling asleep … a brief, bright, flash. I wondered at those times if I had seen a momentary electrical spark occurring between neurons (although no research suggests they work this way) … or … more poetically … whether a stray cosmic ray had collided with a neuron setting off the light show … or even more poetically whether I had witnessed a celestial explosion, perhaps a supernova, somewhere in the cosmos.

I subsequently researched reports of bright lights in the brain. There is a phenomenon, or related phenomena, called "brain zaps", associated with seizure activity or medication withdrawal, particularly with anti-depressants. A person experiencing these phenomena seem to have them

129

with some frequency and often associated with physical unease. Some report a sense of "brain shaking".

My experiences were different from the reports I read, in that my couple of experiences were of a singular brilliant light flash ... all two or three episodes, separated over a number of years ... perhaps one second or less in duration ... and in this most recent experience, because of the tremendous sound that came on the heels of the brilliant flash of light ... a sound that penetrated and reverberated throughtout my body .. just as it would feel if my body had taken the force of a blast.

What does this mean? I have no idea. Meteors crash into the Earth every day, Am I so connected deep in my mind to the world around me that I can "psychically" experience exploding stars, crashing meteorites or the rare collision of a cosmic ray with a singular, unfortunate neuron? Are there explanations for "brain zaps" other than the clinical literature that pathologizes the experience because the research has focused only on individuals with clinical conditions? How many "normal" people have this experience without the correlated seizure, medication, or other medical conditions?

Just recently I became aware that NASA has been studying the reason that astronauts in space report seeing flashes of light in their minds. The current understanding is that this intercranial light show is the result of high energy particles passing through their brains. This surprising phenomenon may support my personal hypothesis about my own experience with exploding pinpoints of light in my own mind down here on the surface of the Earth.

I suspect I will never have an answer to this question. Nevertheless, it reconfirms, as do so many other personal experiences, that a concentrated awareness, which I call "myself", continues to have an observational and reactional life inside my brain, even when the brain itself is in a state we know as "sleep" ... and this awareness is often left puzzled by what it has experienced.

A Taste of Infinity

My personal experience and research have convinced me that a major problem in human psychology is the fusion of sense-of-self with one's beliefs, thoughts, and reactions. Without the recognition ... and an occasional direct experience of ... being *something aware inside the body* ... while the body is producing emotion-influencing chemicals and trains of associational thinking ... it is inevitable that we will assume that what we are, at our core, is these thoughts, reactions, and sensations. This creates the illusion that I know who and what I am and that my reactions to people and events are an accurate expression of my true nature, rather than a pattern of reactions triggered by conditioned cues masquerading as a free and independent person.

The aim of transformational psychology, whether in the form of a religious practice or depth psychotherapy or the great meditative traditions, is to unveil what lies behind my habits of thought, emotional reaction, and physical postures. What is the experience of Self when I am momentarily free from these conditioned patterns which I assume are myself?

There are three historical approaches to such training. First, one can learn to become free of the belief that one is only one's body, by developing the Will to go against the body's preferences for comfort and avoidance of discomfort. This freedom, when one chooses to exercise it, brings into the forefront the recognition that I am in an intimate relationship with my body but that it has a mind of its own, infinitely faster and more complex than I am able to follow. I am a passenger aware inside my body, but I am not my body.

Second, one can learn to develop Will in relation to one's emotional preferences, likes and dislikes, so that one is free to choose without being in thrall to the passion of the moment. This allows me to recognize that there are molecular fluctuations within my body and nervous system which give rise to labels I have been conditioned to associate with certain sensations, such as anxiety or relaxation or excitement or revulsion or attraction. But, by experiencing *Self as a Witness* to these feelings, I can come to a recognition and capacity to not automatically act upon them. This frees me from their conditioned grip.

Third, one can learn to observe thoughts and their patterns associated with different situations, to recognize that since I can observe and examine such associational thought flows, I, as the Witness, am not the thoughts.

Since my sense of self is substantially based on accepting these patterns as representative of who and what I believe I am ... to become free of this belief ... but also to witness the reality of its deception in a moment ... changes the understanding of who and what I may be. What could I experience if my sense of self was freed from all its conditioned associations? This is another way of asking who am I behind the veil of personality and a lifetime of self-image building? To deepen this search for the space beyond the ordinary sense of self, I decided to enroll in a short-term course of Ketamine treatment.

Ketamine is a dissociative drug frequently used as an anesthetic. Its potential to treat depression, PTSD and other psychological/emotional disorders is just now beginning a period of active research and application. I contacted a nearby Ketamine clinic and arranged for a two-hour session with a physician who would administer and monitor the process throughout.

I was asked what I was seeking from this encounter. I replied that I wanted to have the experience of being beyond my ego, beyond my personality, beyond any associations connected with the personage I knew as Steve. It was decided to start off with a small oral dose for me to begin the ... descent? ... ascent? ... into the outer reaches of my mind in a gradual manner. The first fifteen minutes immediately produced a very powerful body high. My senses were acutely heightened, and my body began to move and twitch involuntarily.

At the quarter hour mark, a larger intramuscular dose was administered. Now my senses were so heightened that the music and the Tibetan singing bowls I had brought to set a mood, became overwhelmingly stimulating. The energy coursing through my body was nearly too much to bear. My guide decided I was "stuck" and offered a booster dose to move the experience to a different level. The additional injection was administered.

My situation changed almost immediately. Up until this time I had been aware of the room surrounding me and my guide sitting next to me. Now there was no sense of my body, which until that moment had been so uncomfortably distracting in its sensitivity, but my emotional energy was now even more agitated. I presumed my guide was still with me, but I had no sense of his physical presence. My perceptual field was filled with floating "shards" ... I don't know of what ... it was as if something hard had shattered into many razor-sharp triangular pieces. In one of them floating above my location was a tiny, bright, pinpoint light.

My voice seemed to emanate some distance away from me ... as if it were coming from my feet. The voice was labored. It was repeatedly expressing; "Where am I? What's happening? Who am I? What is this place? I don't understand what's happening. Am I o.k.? Will I come back?" My guide's responses were reassuring. I have no sense of how long I was inside this phase.

Then, something changed. All the agitation ceased. It was still and silent. I became aware of stars. I was *in* "outer space" perceptually. My mind began to view the galaxy ... then became aware of more galaxies beyond. It had opened to a totally new experience. My emotional mood shifted. I *felt the reality* of our human situation ... tiny, flickering life forms on a tiny planet floating in an *Infinite* Universe. I felt ...I *experienced* ... the reality of Eternity and Infinity. The experience was terrifying! I heard a deep, heart-rending moan begin in my chest and move down my body to exit as sound far away near my feet. After several of these guttural utterances of overwhelmed astonishment, I became aware of a scream building itself up behind the moans. I felt the scream, still externally silent but building towards a crescendo in my mind, beginning to move towards its escape point at the bottom of my body. I was aware of a concern that it would be so loud as to disturb the entire clinic in which this was taking place. When it finally emerged, it felt and sounded overwhelming to me, but later my guide assured me that it was powerful but not as loud as it had seemed to me.

To try to describe this further, I had never felt terror like this in my life ... but it was no ordinary terror of a very strong nature. It was not a fear of physical death. It was, rather, an overwhelming recognition of my ... or our ... incomprehensible insignificance in the face of such ineffable enormity. Yet "I", despite my infinitesimal size in relation to the Whole, was still there ... here? ... to experience this felt existential understanding. This was ... was the experience of true *Awe* ... perhaps akin to the Old Testament phrase, *"Fear of the Lord"*. I had touched the edge of Eternal Infinity ... I *felt* ... I *experienced* the truth of its *reality* ... it was not an idea or thought or concept, but an actual direct experience ... and I realized that this was an experience the human mind was not designed to be able to digest. I had gone as far out as I possibly could and found, what seemed to me, at the moment, the human limit ... at least for this human.

Subjectively, this moment of confrontation was very brief, perhaps less than a minute. I was surprised to find myself beginning to feel "normal" again. I complained to my guide that I thought this experience was supposed to last two hours and it felt like only a half hour or so had transpired. He assured me that I had been in this altered state for the full two hours.

I quote now from a debriefing communication with my guide a few days later:

> "Initially I assumed in the peak moment of the experience that I was face-to-face with the Universe. A couple of days later, I realized I could also have found myself face-to-face with the interior of my brain ... or mind. Following the sense of this, then led to a viewing of the entire experience that proceeded the Encounter as labor pains. The fracturing may have been a visual representation of either my sense-of-self "coming apart" or the experience of being awake inside a brain where the normal connections are firing differently ... or not as much ... or not at all. Then, my awareness was "birthed" directly into the face of the Immensity.

> One take away from this stage of the experience is that the familiar awareness of myself as the experiencer continues even under such severe and chaotic distortions in brain functioning. My complaints that I could not orient myself... *"Where am I? What is this place? What is happening?"* ... attest to a continuity of a feeling of myself that is common to all my experiences of being in a conscious state, of being aware of myself as the Witness.

> The familiar taste of that state is what I most associate with a sense of "self" ... the subjective experience of being aware ... but *not my labels or roles or life stories* ... the latter being veri-

fied by my utterances at this time of, *"Who am I? What am I?*

I had no references for myself other than the impression being experienced at that moment. I do not recall a connection with my physical body at that point, although the sensations associated with the turbulence were present up to the moment before the confrontation. At this later stage they seemed more of an emotional and mental disturbance rather than physical. And the profound shock in the moment of confrontation, the emotional sensation which accompanied the awe and terror, must have been biochemically induced by my experiential recognition of ... first, my awareness of being tossed about in a totally alien space and ... secondly, the shock at the moment of confrontation. The shock involved the experiential recognition of my profound insignificance in the face of this infinite vastness ... but also the reaffirmation of the existence of my awareness even under those self-annihilating circumstances.

The theme of a relationship between inner and outer space, the mind as an inherent part of the Universe, as a quality of the quantum realm, has been the object of my research and exploration for some time now. It has recently culminated in some extensive writing about this theme. So ... is this my mind showing me what I am already interested in ... has my interest directed the outcome ... or is this experience only one of infinite ways that the Ultimate appears to individuals according to the lens or model, scientific or religious or philosophical, that they look through? In any case, the experience was a way of showing me what I suspect, that Mind and the Void are somehow connected.

Another analogy that later came, was being lifted on a rocket towards space ... shuddering violently, resisted by gravity ... only to pop out of the atmosphere into a silent, still, immensity ... and then a few moments later arcing back into the atmosphere for the descent back to Earth without sufficient time to look around once free of gravity.

I shared this with a few colleagues and was asked if I felt differently. In a subtle way I did. Somehow, at least for a while, I felt more solid, quieter, whole, present.

I am feeling now that the moment of confrontation with that great Something, is the peak experience of my life. Memory of *that moment visits me now many times a day. Although part of me is, at the moment, reluctant to put itself again through that violently energetic experience, what lay just beyond it is now firmly fixed in me as my central, haunting question. Perhaps, as many women forget about the pain once the child is born, this queasiness about going through the disorientation will weaken as the pull of continuing this exploration strengthens ... and/or the next time, if it is similar, having been through those stages already, perhaps I won't be as disturbed by the disorientation and better able to focus.*

It was a very good idea to take time for the experience to be processed. This afternoon I realized the experience did succeed in bringing me to my goal. I was so distracted by the energy and confusion that I just recognized that after the "splintering" experience I then was in front of the Unnamable, Unbearable reality which was emotionally overwhelming and led to my moaning-scream of awe. Perhaps if I had been able to stabilize at that point and had a bit more time .... nevertheless, in retrospect, you did get me there. Now, if the energy could be less violent on the way there ......"

A number of months later I returned for a second experience. The process was identical but without the initial oral warm-up period. I encountered the same jarring energy in my body as before. Although being somewhat familiar with the experience of this drug, I was again distracted by the degree of body agitation. Then my field of awareness altered. Although I recognized that part of me wished to return to the edge of Infinity once more ... and this time for a longer time to look around ... I also knew that something different might happen. Now, instead of the recognizable image of the Universe, I found myself confronted with an endless field of hierarchies of overlapping, interactive, geometric forms and shapes ... an infinity of them. Again, my voice seemed to emerge from my feet far away from me, asking my guide, "It is so vast! How can I take it all in? It is ... SO ... BIG ...! Can I remain sane? How can I hold this all?"

Again, I was confronted with the *experiential taste* and *feel* of *Infinitude*. Reflecting later on this experience, it seemed to me that I had been taken into the Micro-Universe to be confronted by impressions symbolic of the underlying world of atoms and sub-atomic particles. It was not a thought. It was a direct experience.

136

Given my training as a psychologist, it is legitimate to ask, as I did of myself following the first encounter, whether the geometry of my mind and its interests contributed either to the impressions and/or my interpretation of them. This may be very likely but does nothing to diminish the impact of these experiences. Historically, many different seers, saints, mystics, and philosophers have been confronted with this reality in ways resonant with their idiosyncratic world view. Just as we tend to think with the words that our language provides us, we also associate with the images our culture has given us. Sometimes, the experience is so far beyond our conditioning that we are left struggling to find words or unable to even draw what we have seen. The difference in form is not important. What is important is the similarity with the reported state of Awe/Terror and the changing of sense of self and reality as a result of the confrontation.

What did I learn from this experience? I recognize that despite catastrophic disorientation in my perceptual field, the familiar sense of I, myself as Observer, the taste of personal awareness, remained even though contact with my body and surrounds disappeared. It raises for me a way of thinking about how something could perhaps survive the death of the body. I had repeatedly exclaimed, in the midst of the disorientation, "Where am *I*? Who am *I*? How can *I* hold all this within my infinitesimal self?" If this phenomenon we call *I*, can hold itself together while all else around it is disintegrating, perhaps it is a *something* related to this mysterious Observer, the Experiencer who recognizes the familiar taste of himself even when he is beyond name and self-recognition.

As Inside, So Outside; As Above, So Below

Quotations

"Consciousness cannot be accounted for in physical terms. For consciousness is absolutely fundamental. It cannot be accounted for in terms of anything else."

Erwin Schrödinger

"The laws of nature are but the mathematical thoughts of God."

– Euclid

"The absence of evidence is not evidence of absence."

Carl Sagan

As Inside, So Outside; As Above, So Below

God at the Synapse

We hang suspended ... and if conscious ... crucified ... as a bridge between the material world and the world from which originates the code which has programed our existence.

For me, the path first revealed itself ... and continues to call me ... through the mystery of: Where am I the moment before I awake? Who roams my inner mansion searching for the way back home? Who wakes me? Who calls me? Who already lives there ...in my future ... waiting for the rest of me to arrive?

Fact: *"Immensely complex levels of digestion begin at the interface with the world and end at the cortex ... and occupy in the time of neural integration synaptic associative and reverberation a whole 0.5 seconds. Within this half second however and before we know it by cortical activation, a gamut of ever widening streams of relationship is explored and completed. Synaptic relays can occupy as short an interval as 0.004 seconds. At each synapse it is now thought that a neuron can then share that information, in thousandths of a second, with three to 5000 other neurons. Throughout that half second interval man is not aware, has no higher cortical activation, of what is going on as the sensory interface moves upward through the hierarchy of centers on its way to man's cortex. It is evident that the vast majority, if not all, of these patterns of integration association are prewired'.**

This sequence involves only the *sensory input*! It does not address the complexification of ongoing regulatory functions ... nor the higher cortical functions ... the complexity of ongoing processes operating from womb through our entire lives is ... for all practical purposes ... infinite. All this happens, *factually* and *verifiably*, inside our

---

* *The Neurophysiology of Television Viewing: a Preliminary Report*, Keith Buzzell, DO, unpublished manuscript.

central nervous system. It can be measured and tracked.

Something is in continual movement! *Something* ... some energy ... exists inside of us that flows through the endless connections and combinations of neural pathways and is omnipresent inside the universe of our nervous system. When this 'something' reaches our brain stem ... then our midbrain ... and then our cortex ... *we become aware* of what exists *in that location* ... the viewpoint, memories, agendas ... of that part of the brain which has been illuminated ... activated ... energized ...by the touch of this 'something'.

We know the structure of nerve cells. We know how electrical currents move through them. We know that a 'wave' of 'something' causes sodium and potassium ions to rapidly switch places from inside the axon sheath to outside and back again along the length the neuronal axon. When that 'wave' reaches the end of the neuron, if of sufficient intensity ... the all or nothing principle ... it stimulates the production, and/or release, of over 60 different specialized transmitter molecules at last count ... that "float' across the vast ... from the molecule's perspective ... *space* between the axon and the dendritic receiving fibers of the next neuron. At the next neuron, the transmitter molecules will influence the initiation of a 'wave' depending on their many possible combinations and levels of concentration. How many combinations and permutations are there of 60 different energetic qualities ... without factoring the infinite variety of differing concentration levels?

In the central nervous system, we are within the world of molecules and inside that, the world of atoms and electrons. What is it that programs these molecules and electrons to bob and weave along the crest of the invisible wave? What is encoded in the pattern of the wave that produces the phenomena of thought and feeling and awareness? What is it that moves the wave into motion? We are in the vast universe of moving molecules and inside of these, an even faster universe of flip-flopping electrons. Where in these interlocking, interactive universes do we locate thought, feeling, hope, wish, or fear ... and the sense of ... I?

As we peer into the synapse, we look past the world of materiality. There are no nerve cells in the space. This space is empty. Yet the space is filled with the vibration that moves the energy that lights up our nervous system that allows millions of simultaneous homeostatic functions to occur from conception to death and all materializing prior to reaching the level of conscious awareness. And conscious awareness, itself, must leap the gulf of the synapse to continue its flow along the pipeline of a trillion pathways.

Where in this verifiable matrix of matter and flowing energy am I ... are you? Where does insight originate? What is a Wish and how does it become translated through billions of neuronal layers to appear in enactment as manifested muscular activity? Who is it that is wishing? Where is this "Wisher" located? Where are the layers ....Where are the layers of consciousness that psychotherapists believe they can see and manipulate?

What is the ladder we are climbing inside our nervous system when we move upward ... or inwards ... if one prefers that metaphorical 'direction' ... towards greater perspective, deeper understanding, a more centered viewing of ourselves? Where are the sub personalities? Where the demons? Where are the angels? Where is "Real I"? Where is Ego? Where is the Soul? We appear to exist in the pattern of electrical activity in a world beyond the individual molecules, beyond the electrons and atoms that move within us.

I think ... I feel ... I sense. ...I hope ... I dream ... therefore I am. But where am I and what am I? The mystery of me is not just poetic and metaphorical. I can see and verify the literalness of my mystery just by looking inside myself and seeing that I am looking into the synaptic void to try and catch a glimpse of what is looking out of the void trying to see itself in me.

As Inside, So Outside; As Above, So Below

Awareness and the Avatar
A Fable

O nce upon a time there was an Awareness. It was aware of itself, but there was nothing else ... no other thing for it to become aware of. It seemed to be all alone. It wanted to understand itself. What was it? Where was it? What was its purpose for being aware of itself?

Since its awareness-of-being-aware seemed to be all that there was, it wondered where it could look to increase its knowledge and understanding of itself. It realized that, since at the least, it was aware that it existed for itself, the only way of search would be to deepen that awareness of itself. Was there anything else inside itself to become aware of? It would need some source of comparison, certainly a source of new perspective to add to the field of attention in which Awareness found itself.

Then Awareness noticed something. It was *not* entirely alone. There were *thoughts* in its field of awareness ... thoughts about wondering what it was and the reason for its being aware. Then it noticed something else. There were *emotions*. It *wished* to know, it *longed* to know.

At first, Awareness wondered where the thoughts and the wish were where coming from. "Is *that* what I am", it wondered ... "awareness, thoughts and a wish?" After giving its attention to this new question, it came to the conclusion that the thoughts and wish must be a part of itself, since they were now encompassed by the light of its attention ... but they could *not* be it, itself in total, as it had been aware of itself before the thoughts and their attendant emotion had appeared in its sphere of awareness. It reasoned further, that since it could *be aware of* the thoughts and emotion, it, itself, must be more than ... if not something different from ... what it was noticing. *Awareness, thoughts,* and *feeling* must be different qualities within a single field of attention.

Now Awareness reasoned that, although it was not entirely alone, as it now had the company of its thoughts and a wish, still nothing was appearing to help illuminate its questions, since the answers were not contained in its own thoughts and feelings. Where else could it look?

Awareness now reasoned that all it had to work with was the attention generated by ... or generating ...its awareness. It could search with its *attention*, but where would it direct its attention to find more about itself? It realized that it needed something else, something *beyond awareness of itself* and its own internal processes, to provide a mirror for feedback to help with its self-study.

Up to this point in our story, only *questions* and a *wish* had been noticed in field of awareness. Then, out of-nowhere, an *idea* appeared for the first time. The idea arose as a response to the initial questions but, strangely, appeared in the form of a *new question*. Could there actually be something ... anything ... beyond awareness of itself? It was assuming the current sense of itself was all there was to experience ... but was that accurate? It would have to look still deeper into the darkness within.

Awareness became very still ... focused inside itself ... and began to ponder. "Where had this idea come from? It felt like it came from "out-of-nowhere". Where was the "place" of "nowhere"? The idea had not initially been in the field of attention ... and then it was. It just appeared! It obviously must have come out of the ... darkness ... the *seeming nothingness* beyond its awareness!

This new idea suggested to Awareness that it could take a portion of its attention and direct that quality deeper into the unknown, unilluminated regions of itself without losing contact with the known. This suggestion carried another realization. Awareness had more than its capacity for attention, thought and feeling. It also had the ability of *initiation*. It could *Will* the direction of attention if it chose to do so. It added this to its small list of discoveries: *awareness, attention, thoughts, feelings* and *willed initiation* ... and the hidden dimension of Nothingness.

Awareness concentrated its attention again, focused it inwards, and exhaled it into the darkness of its interior, beyond the circumference of the light of its current attentional field... and waited ... and waited ... patiently maintaining its gaze into the darkness without losing the experience of itself as the one looking. As its attention penetrated the Nothingness, condensations of the stream of attention began to collect together and become little 'packets', little 'vehicles', each containing an aspect of the awareness of the Awareness. These began to attract other congregations of attention packets and as these adhered to each other they began to organize into Forms.

These first Forms carried the quality of the original Awareness since they were directly made of particles of the Awareness Itself. At first, these initial coalescing Forms were very rarified in their nature, having not required too many particles or packets to take a shape. Their rarefication also meant that their potency was nearly identical to that of the Great Awareness itself. It was as if Awareness had divided into countless fragment of itself, each a particle of its attention.

As these accumulated, the packets squeezed tighter and tighter together. As each was a container carrying the potency of Awareness itself, the accumulating light grew brighter and brighter, and the area of the blending brightness became warmer and warmer and then hotter and hotter until its light burst the darkness of the Nothingness. More and more of these concentrating areas of accumulating particles of Attention appeared until the Nothingness was speckled with the first Forms, three-dimensional globes radiating the energy of their source.

Awareness realized that the radius of its attention was expanding, as each particle, coalescing with others into the round Forms carrying its awareness, was at the same time, an extension of itself moving outward in all directions into the limitless Nothingness. In doing so, it could inhabit the newly arising Forms. It could direct its attention through them, into the level of these newly emerging materializations … a world 'below' itself, as Awareness, itself, was formless.

With the light of its attention now shining *through* these newly condensed glowing globes or 'windows', it could look out into the vastness of the Nothingness which was now illuminated by an infinite and continually increasing number of glowing lights. Thus Awareness enlarged the field of its attention throughout the expanding light which began to fill the darkness of the Nothingness. Whatever came to its attention through all these illuminated representatives of itself was now absorbed and digested into its deepening understanding.

As the radii of all the shining globes expanded simultaneously in all directions, soon the ripples of widening light began to overlap. After a while, all of the Nothingness was saturated with light and became a single field of illumination filled with Attention originating from above its level. The field of attention occupied by Awareness had expanded its circumference exponentially. It was now in direct contact with all the emerging Forms, as it was inhabiting them, and using them as platforms of its continuing search. Whatever information lay in this newly created world within the expanding field of noticing and watching, was conveyed instantly into Awareness through this continual exchange with these extensions of itself.

Then, around these 'glowing windows' through which Awareness was watching, other, denser, concentrations arose. These were made from a combination of the original particles, which had not become part of the shining lights, and some which had been processed inside the bright balls and then breathed out again into the Nothingness. Because these secondary Forms were made of a combination of particles of slightly different levels, both coming directly and indirectly from the Source, they were of greater density of mass and less potency than the shining lights.

These remaining particles also formed three-dimensional shapes, but, due to their mixture and smaller size, they did not have sufficient capacity to produce light of their own. They lived in the reflected light of the attention streaming from their nearest shining 'representative' of The Great Awareness.

Awareness now found itself gazing out into this new world of Forms appearing beyond the original circle of its awareness. For a moment, it wondered if this newly noticed world had always existed but was only now being discovered because attention had been directed inward ... or had these Forms come into existence only when Attention gazed into the Nothingness? Did its Attention bring these new forms into existence just by the effort to look or had there always been something beyond itself of which it was only now becoming aware?

Once again, a new thought had popped into its field of attention from beyond the boundary of its awareness a moment before. It had no way to determine the answer to this new question. It seemed as if the more it paid attention and expanded its awareness, the more questions appeared. But as Awareness maintained its gaze, it still could not find anything to help in its quest for understanding itself and its purpose, as all the newer, denser Forms now appearing in the Nothingness ...below the level of the illuminated windows ... were dark, unable to generate their own light.

More Forms of different density began to each occupy their own "level" ... so that layers ... or worlds ... of different densities began to appear in the expanding circumference of the Breath of Awareness

These non-self-illuminating Forms still carried the essence of the Creative Awareness but were further and further "removed" in potency due to their greater density, compared with the ultimate purity of the Initiating Awareness. The greater the density, the more that density interfered with the vibratory potency coming down from above their level. As a result, each level and quality of "density" carried with it, and manifested, different functional capacities and potentialities.

Even though there were now uncountable infinities of concentrations through which Awareness extended itself, still nothing could be discovered that could help in its quest for understanding and purpose. As these layers of its Universe developed, Awareness realized it could continue to expand the circle of its attention into all the Forms at the different levels, so that each infinitesimal particle would carry a crystal of its own attention ... embedded inside every particle ... inside each Form. Therefore, as coalescing Forms proliferated, so did the expanding and deepening circle of Awareness.

Thus, each Form became a compartment, a tiny 'home' for an aspect of the attention of Awareness through which it could search for the answer to its questions; "What am I? What is my purpose"? But look and look, search and search as it might, through the growing, and densifying, ever expanding coalescence of particles of its own light, it could not find the answer. All it found was an awareness of itself looking for the reason for itself.

What to do? Awareness understood that it was still only talking with itself. It was still trapped inside the circle of its own awareness, which, although continually expanding and occupying an infinity of Forms, had not yet been able to find anything existing, except reflections of itself. There was no new light coming back from this denser level to bring any new information. It seemed to be the line where the darkness and light first balanced ... before the light began to weaken in its fight with increasing density.

What to do now? Awareness had believed it had now been able to search to the bottom of the multi-dimensioned material Universe it discovered within itself. It had created motion with the expansion of its attention ...but not yet found the answer to its questions.

Now another new recognition appeared in its understanding. It realized it needed help; it needed a new source of light that could bring a perspective different from its own. But ... if it was the only Awareness in existence, what could help it gather more impressions around its haunting questions?

Another new thought suddenly appeared, again, apparently out of nowhere. Awareness thought to itself, that what was needed was an *additional* source of *semi-independent awareness* to carry the Light at these lower levels. It needed different types of Forms ... 'vehicles' ... in this lower dimension which could both contain ... but also magnify ... the Light of its attention. If these Forms were going to actively help in the search, they would have to have their own initiative and curiosity to notice what was happening around them and go investigate. These new Forms would have to carry an aspect of the Creative Impulse as well as the in-dwelling light of Attention. They would need to be Forms which could contain miniaturized versions of the qualities of Awareness implanted inside them. These could serve as semi-autonomous representatives of the Initiating Awareness ... each a single photon of the original.

These semi-independent Forms would require an animating energy that would give them the required qualities. They would have to be able to contain the energy that they, themselves, would eventually give the name of "Life". This life-energy would endow them with the capacity to be active and sensitive in relation to the level of dimensions, or "worlds", in which their Life was destined to manifest.

Awareness then first created Forms that could contain Life and would therefore be able to sense and interact with their environment. Awareness fed these tiny living machines with energy from particles of its attention, flowing through the nearest illuminating portal, or Star. Fed by particles of light, these now *'living' Forms took in this energy and transformed it inside themselves.* Some of this transformed energy refueled the Life within them, and, just as the energy of attention was sent out from Awareness ... through the stars ... to become a source of energy-food for other different types of Life Forms appearing on the Planets ... now the Life Forms also emanated from themselves ... energy ... both transformed and not digestible by them ... and that transformation became nutrient for other living-machines in the surrounding environment which could eat what others did not need or could not digest. Everything at this new level of Life was now constantly exchanging energy with others' energies ... all originating from Awareness and coming to them through their Sun. And this energy was the Light of the Attention of Awareness.

But these little machines still did not sufficiently magnify the tiny Light inside themselves, coming from far Above. Awareness could only perceive what the little machines could be aware of, as their field of attention was very circumscribed. Bigger, better, more complex machines with greatly expanded capacities for Awareness were needed.

A new *quality of experience* now appeared in the field of the attention of Awareness. These new Life Forms were endowed with a quality of energy which allowed them, through their bodies, to *experience an exchange of vibrations* from their surroundings. They had become sensitive to the taste and feel of the world, both around and inside their material Form.

Awareness was delighted to recognize that, through these Life Forms, it also could now have the understanding derived by experiencing through a body. In fact, it discovered that the experience of sensations continually gathered through the bodies of these Life Forms, was generating energy for Awareness to help intensify its search. It realized it could "farm" the experiences of living things to enhance its own expanding understanding. As these living things were an extension of itself, Awareness realized the life forms were feeding energy from their experiences back to the greater Awareness that was connected to them.

Awareness recognized that it was adding to its growing list of qualities, discovered inside its circle of existence: attention, thought, feeling, will and now *sensation*.

These questions burned so intensely that Awareness felt forced to create a multi-dimensional Universe to accommodate its every expanding search. It also realized that it needed to understand its feelings about these questions. Why did they feel so very important? It, itself had no mass-based body, being but pure Awareness, yet it was experiencing thoughts and feelings.

It realized that since it experienced Feeling and Thought, those aspects of itself would also be carried within the beam of its Attention. The Universe it had set in motion must also have feeling and intellectual levels, just as it, itself, did ... in addition to sensations experienced by living materialized Forms. But were the Forms capable of experiencing at the levels of thought and feeling that could correspond to these aspects of The Awareness?

Perhaps the missing information Awareness sought might be at those levels rather than the dense material and the physical forms of living bodies. Maybe the answers it sought dwelt in the realm of feeling and higher conceptualization. What could give new perspective on Emotion and Intellect? It needed higher Life Forms that could process, digest, and transmit emotional and intellectual experiences, in addition to sensory.

These more complex Forms, (later to be known as animals), gradually developed increasing degrees of intelligence and problem-solving as well as an emotional life focused on family, play, sex, and exploration. In the animals, sensation was now joined by an emotional life which filled Awareness with deeper, richer experiences. But the machinery of the animals was not yet complex enough to access and process information from the conceptual realms. Still greater degrees of both intellect and subtleties of emotion were required.

Another new thought appeared in Awareness. It realized it needed assistants, living, *self-conscious* Forms that it could communicate with and direct to help it in its search. It needed Forms in some way similar to itself in their capacity to be aware that their existence straddled at least three different levels: intellect, emotion and physical sensation.

What was needed was a still higher Life Form that could become aware of its own existence as the receiver of impressions from these three levels of sensation, emotion, and intellect. This Life Form, this most complex of machines, would have the potential for cognizant awareness of communication across the levels. This Form would serve as an *Avatar* and become a representative of Awareness on the surface of the Cosmic Forms called Planets. This Avatar* had to have the potential to experience the mystery of its own existence so that it could share in the *desire* of Awareness.

This Avatar, later called human, was a different kind of animal, a different kind of Life Form. The human had the potential to sense the existence of Awareness inside itself and, by choice and decision, to open to Awareness, so it could work as a partner, even knowing that this process would forever change the human into something entirely different, that this submission would transform the human-animal into a true *Hu-man†*

---

* Avatar: an incarnation in human form/ an embodiment (as of a concept or philosophy) often in a person / an electronic image that represents and may be manipulated by a computer user (as in a game)

† Hu is God in Sanskrit. "Hu-man" = God-man as distinct from "human" = man not connected with the Divine.

... a blended God-infused-human.

Up until this point, all of life had been a *passive* transformer and transmitter of experiences of different vibrations, feeding both itself and ... unconsciously ... the watchful eye of Awareness. The human had the potential to be an *active* transmitter and magnifier ... to develop into a Hu-man. The Hu-man would have the potency to understand and intentionally transform and upgrade the energy carried within the vibrations streaming through it at all times which it called "impressions of experience". The Hu-man could search for and create its own sense of Meaning. It could become a *creator* of new conceptual understandings at a higher dimensional level of experience. The Hu-man would have the capacity to resolve paradox and become a reconciling force, a new power for the transmission of the Light of Awareness out into its own world, while simultaneously assisting in the search for meaning desired by Awareness itself ... above ... and deep within. If Hu-mans could appear from the mass of humans, then there would finally be a new source of Understanding to feed the quest of Awareness.

The Hu-man was to be an Avatar, designed to consciously carry the representative of Awareness, extended down, down, down into the increasingly dense layers of the Universe it had created in order to help answer its questions. Awareness now began to *taste* experiences through these new self-initiating representatives of itself, the Hu-man. And the Hu-man now became *sensitive, inside itself*, to what it called, the 'I', or the Observer or the Witness, the Presence, or the Soul.

And it was this successful subjective blending of levels that led a new problem to take root.

The Observer, the *representative* of Awareness, became fascinated with being able to experience Life from inside a thinking, feeling, sensing, reasoning Form ... a Form now reflecting its own creative qualities. It became so mesmerized by the multi-dimensional experiencing capacity of the Hu-man that it kept falling "asleep", forgetting to be aware of itself in the mesmerizing flow of Life. In those moments of forgetting its source, this embodied Avatar came instead to believe that it, itself, was only the machine with its attached personality and conditioned reactions. It forgot that it originated above that ordinary mechanical human level in order to utilize this machine as a search engine as well as an experience-producing generator. But even more challenging was the fact that every time it fell into the trance of self-forgetfulness, the Hu-man also lost its conscious connection with its higher origins and devolved back into a human-animal, unaware of the in-dwelling Awareness.

When 'awake' to itself, momentarily free from the hypnotism of stimulation and mechanical reactions, the Observer would describe the state as like finding itself inside a 'computer game', a 'virtual reality' experience, like a lucid dream. The Observer would know it was awake inside the Avatar, inside the dream. And with the shock of this remembrance, the human would transform into its Hu-man level of perception, understanding and experience.

Because it was attached to a body through its Avatar, Awareness could now move around the physical world at the material level of existence. It would have to protect the body, or at least not interfere with the body's innate programming to protect itself. When awake, the Observer could watch the machinery of the personality which had been programmed into the Avatar's computer by exposure to surrounding life. This separate awareness of itself inside the Avatar would continually remind the Observer that it was only able to participate at this higher level through the relationship with Attention from Above.

Participation of the Observer would have to establish some distance from what it was experiencing in order to avoid falling asleep in the dream and becoming identified with the body and personality it was occupying. This necessitated continual awareness of itself inside the Avatar. And ... if the Avatar could become aware of itself through the higher energy of the Observer, then the two would momentarily merge ...the Avatar would now be awake to its true nature, as long as the connection of recognition lasted. It would then access the experience of its Hu-man potential, the human who knows it carries the light of its creator inside itself.

Now, yet again, another difficulty arose. In addition to the hypnotic effect of continuous sensory, emotional, and mental stimulation, there was another reason the Observer so often fell asleep inside its human Avatar. The more fixed the patterns of stimulus-response reactions conditioned into the Avatar by its unbroken exposure to Life, the noisier and more unbalanced and more turbulent was the state of the emotional/mental energy inside the Avatar. When the small circle of awareness inside a human was cluttered with conditioned emotional/ mental/ physical patterns, it became denser and more opaque and thus a less potent transmitting and processing machine than it should have been. It was often so loud and busy inside the Avatar that the Observer could not hear itself think and the Avatar could not notice the still, small voice of Presence trying to guide it and ask for its help in searching for answers to the questions posed by Higher Awareness.

Because of these difficulties, The Observer, the representative of Awareness, had to continually struggle to try to remember itself and its mission. It had to struggle to separate its sense-of-itself and its purpose from the Avatar's computerized personality, idiosyncratic sense-of-itself and its subjective, individualized, life-oriented goals and wishes.

As the Witness could not do this alone, it needed to stabilize the help it could receive from the Avatar. The Observing-Witness was always connected with its Source, but that connection grew weaker under the hypnotic pull of the demands of the life in the body and personality. There was one other adjustment needed. Awareness realized it must not only make the body and personality of the Avatar aware of its existence inside themselves, but it also needed the Avatar to make its own efforts to free itself from its own conditioned patterns so that the Witnessing-Presence could introduce the Avatar to its true nature and purpose. To do so, the human had to learn how to increase the drop of Will it had received from Above which resided inside all the light-carrying particles buried within its Form.

The Witness hoped that when the Avatar realized its true nature ... that it was a machine with the possibility of becoming more than a machine ... then it would willingly cooperate with the Observer in order to serve Awareness. Then the Avatar would understand its own purpose in the larger scale and become a helpful servant in the quest of Awareness for its identity and purpose. The Avatar would open itself to the Presence within it and draw on that energy to increase its little bit of will-to-struggle to "stay awake" and share in the search.

The Witness inside then listened and studied the interior subjective experience of each Avatar. From that listening emanated the Witness's *wish* for contact. The wish created a reverberation in the minds and feelings of humans. Some of the more sensitive humans heard and felt this wish and began to resonate with it. These humans began to wake up from their sleep, thus beginning the path of transformation towards becoming Hu-man. Using the power of the Witness within them, they now also began to study their own thoughts, feelings, reactions in the hope of learning how they *themselves* were programmed.

This power brought the ability to separate the sense-of-themselves from the functions ongoing inside of them which they had previously believed to be all that they were. The Avatar began to wake up inside itself, momentarily free from its animal and human programming.

The vibrations, now shared together by the human Avatar and its indwelling Presence, began to awaken the sleeping potential inside such Avatars. They felt a Presence inside them and wanted to open to its influence. Under this prompting, the awakening Avatar began to reason differently. For a moment, the Avatar could escape its conditioned program and, as its mind stilled and its heart opened under the warming effect of the Witnessing-Presence, it began to wonder. Under the influence of this opening connection with a higher world, the awakening Avatars began to ask questions of themselves. They began to wonder, "Who am I? What am I? What is my purpose?"

Now, Awareness, through its representative Witness inside an awakened Hu-Man, could resume its search at a deeper level of its Creation. Hoping that this advanced Avatar might be able to discover a new understanding, it now listened intently to the Hu-man's thoughts and feelings.

And this is what it heard ….

A Hu-Man Avatar's Musings

> "As Avatars ourselves, those of us who have these wonderings assume they are personal questions … that we think them up ourselves. If these questions begin to drive us, they are important … at least to us. They don't seem to be coming from the life outside. This planet, Earth, is full of life, but there is no evidence that any other Life Form has the capacity to ask such questions … or that there is any need to hold these questions in order to live out a life on our planet.
>
> Looking at all the humans around me, I don't notice many of them asking these questions either. If these are questions coming from my interior world, then the answer must therefore also lie deep inside me.

Something, very, very deep in the interior wants to know ... wants to know very badly. Is *something*, other than myself, asking these questions of me? Is it asking me to ask its questions also? Am I part of its search, while believing it is my search only? Are It and I separate or are we somehow the same?

Is my purpose here on Earth to answer these questions? Who am I answering them for? Whose request am I following? Could these questions actually be coming from 'above' my level and require me to be open and willing to search, from down here at the level of Life, for the answers? That would imply that the answers have not been found on levels above here either! So, my questions may have been put into my head to motivate me to search for a resolution for *That*, above me, which is actually asking Its' questions through me.

How far above me does the questioning go? If Awareness, or the Universe, or God, or Endlessness, or It, already knows who and what and why It is ... why would any part of Its Creation ... all of which carries particles of the Light of Its Awareness ... be unaware of the answer ... since All is connected through the Light?

Maybe the Ultimate Awareness created a multidimensional universe and sent its Attention down, through all the layers to the level of human life, to occupy an Avatar of Its creation, like myself, as a vehicle to move around the planet to seek out an understanding of Its questions. Could it be that Awareness Itself *does not know* the answer to these questions?

Are these God's questions I have been asked to contribute something to? What could I provide that the levels above me lack for themselves? The only thing unique to me are my own experiences. I am the only entity in the Universe who is experiencing life from my idiosyncratic perspective. The geometry of my psyche* is unique. Some spiritual teachings suggest that the shape of my Being, my "spiritual body", may survive the death of my physical body.

What could I discover that the Great Awareness does not already know?

Maybe what I can contribute, what we all can contribute, that

---

* Psyche: the human soul, mind, or spirit.

might be a truly new creation is my idiosyncratic sense of meaning. *If my need to understand what I am and what my purpose is, if these questions are implanted in me from above, then my search for meaning may, itself, be the meaning of my existence.*

As the search for meaning can only take place in the higher psychic dimensions ... and whatever happens in the interior of my Psyche is instantly known to the Witness ... then the experiences of all humans and all living creatures would be simultaneously Witnessed by the collective representatives of the Great Awareness inside each living form. *That would make each of us a cell in a collective mind designed to have experiences, make discoveries and search for meaning.*

Maybe we are here to add to a *Universal Book of Understanding* ... an addition which can only be written by living, feeling, thinking beings.

When I am awakened by the Presence of the Witness, do I become a new representative of the Light of Awareness ... then able to join in Its search? At the level of the Hu-man, am I a representative of the Light of Awareness whose purpose is to understand who and what I am at my level of Life as well as the levels above?

I discover that I can extend Awareness at many levels inside my own personal universe of sensation, memory, thought, wish, impulse, experience. I can send my Attention into my body, into my feelings, into my "thinkings", to discover which come from the conditioning Life around me and which come from another, deeper, higher source that is interested more in the Life within than the Life without.

In a way, the energy of my experiences is not only being digested by myself, but what I digest is then being eaten by the Observing-Presence within me to be transferred up to even higher levels. When I fall into the hypnotism of forgetting my higher nature, I am mostly food for Life. If I am 'awake', I can willingly become food for higher levels that need my experiences to expand their higher dimensional field of awareness.

Further Reflections on Awareness

After listening to this Avatar thought-process, one final idea now appeared in the Cosmic Awareness. As all these experiences of the Life Forms, animal, human and Hu-man, were continually available to the expanding field of Its Attention, the energy of these experiences was also being transferred and blended into Its own expanded scope of Awareness. It realized that as these were accumulating in the Cosmic Psyche, they were forming an ever-expanding library of material for Its own education. Somewhere in all this unique subjective perspective might lie clues to Its questions. It was gratified that Life Forms were serving as crops for the Universal quest. Only a true Hu-man would not regard this as slavery, but a symbiotic relationship of mutual benefit. Only a true Hu-man would be willing to die to the life-generated illusions of itself and joyfully allow itself to be penetrated by, or absorbed into, the worlds above itself. The Hu-man would willingly offer itself as the ultimate food.

Listening to ponderings of such Hu-mans, Awareness was satisfied that It had successfully extended Its Attention, as an experience, as a direct contact, into the living Avatar. Hearing this soliloquy flow through the heart and mind of a Hu-man, Awareness was both gratified and surprised.

Initially, Awareness was gratified because the Avatar now knew itself, and the Witness inside itself, as an extension of The Original Awareness. Now the Hu-man could help in the search for the answers Awareness was seeking. Now, both Awareness and Its Hu-man understood, and could say: "Its questions are my questions because my questions are Its questions; *Who am I? What am I? What is my purpose?*"

But then ... Awareness was shocked ... even dismayed ... by the results of this breakthrough. In finally creating an instrument that could contain a miniaturized version of Its own creative awareness, a psyche in the image-of-Itself, the search seemed to have come full circle.

Awareness had expanded Itself deeper and deeper into the Universe. It had extended Its search, down ... down ... down ... to lower and lower ... and denser and denser levels of existence ...

in search of Its nature and purpose. When Its Avatar, at the level of Life, awakened to the Presence of Awareness inside itself ... the Great Awareness discovered Itself looking back up at Itself asking the same questions, but even now that It had intended to create an independent source of search ... it belatedly realized that inevitably the search would lead back to Itself as the originator of the search. It was not alone. Its Avatar, having failed to find answers to these questions at its own level, was now directing its search back towards the original source of the inquiry. It was now looking upwards toward the great Awareness for the answers which the Great Awareness had created it to solve. Its questions had been heard Below, but were being redirected back to their source. Now, across time and through dimensions higher and lower, reverberated the plaintive call:

"Who am I? What am I? What is my purpose?"

Final Reflections

In concluding this exploration of intuition as a critical instrument for understanding the world and our place in it, I came across two poetic versions of this question written long ago by different versions of my much younger selves. *"Why?"* was conceived in 1964, at age 20. I still clearly recall the moment of writing this and the acute existential pain I was suffering. The second version of this poem, *"Man Watching Stars"*, appeared in the late 1980's, twenty-five or so years later. It demonstrates a sense of deepening, an answer of sorts to the soulful cry of decades earlier.

The accompanying sketch was part of a series of images that came to my mind in my early forties related to this theme. The earliest of these images appear in the first book of this series.* They pictured a man literally rooted to the Earth, his lower legs like tree trunks immobilizing him while, with fists clenched in frustration, he gazed upward crying his question heavenward. Over time, the image changed. The rootedness disappeared and the man stood on his own two feet. Still looking into the night sky, his fists were no longer clenched. A vortex has appeared in the darkness overhead, riveting his gaze.

At the writing of this overview, now forty years onward, an association has just appeared in my mind for the first time. Also, in *The Search for Meaning and the Mystery of Consciousness*, I described the first dream I can recall from around the age of three. In that dream I was looking down into a vortex† and experiencing a feeling of crushing density simultaneously with a feeling of infinite expansion.

It was years later in adulthood that I discovered representations of spirals and vortices which evoked in me the feeling of this first dream. I

---

* *The Search for Meaning and the Mystery of Consciousness: A Psychologists Journey Through Gurdjieff and Jung*, Karnak Press, Austin, Texas, 2022, p. 25
† Technically, a vortex is swirling center of energy that sucks anything near it into itself. In spiritual literature, it is believed to symbolically represent energy that can influence emotional, physical, and spiritual effects.

am now belatedly recognizing the appearance of the vortex in the heavens, at age 40, as a connection with that first dream ... a *revisitation* of *something* that has been accompanying my life from conception.

The foregoing essays in this book represent insights derived subsequent to these earlier expressions and a deepening maturation over the last forty years of search.

Why?

I breathe.

     I sigh.

          I walk.

               I cry.

I am made of tissues and cells, molecules, and atoms.
I am a walking universe of microscopic particles.

My body is alive, my tissues live, my cells are animate,
Yet, the mortar, the building blocks of me do not have life.
Do molecules live?
Are atoms alive?
How can the elements that form blocks of granite, churning oceans and desert sands,

        become alive in me?

I think ... I laugh ... I ponder ...
Yet the trees and rocks do not.
Why?

I reason ... I imagine ... I ponder ...
Yet animals cannot.
Why?
Am I a freak, an accident,
a mutant among the endless stars?

Or is there a design, a scheme, a purpose?

Where am I?
      In a valley,
             on a mountain,
                    by the sea?
Where are these places?

What are these things but ripples or puddles on our tiny planet,
      a rock,
      a pebble,
      a speck of dust,
      a dwindling microbe
Swirling along an endless orb in some far-flung forgotten corner of
the cosmos?

How the stars?
Why the galaxies?
Where is the universe?

Can it be a timeless sea where no clock keeps count,
No pendulum swings,
A bottomless pit where up is down, East is West
And a beam of moonlight gallops off into eternity?
Can there be no end and no beginning?
A ceasing of time and place?

No sound, no wind, no rain …
only silence screaming from the darkness
As icy cold fingers of Starlight stab out from its depths.

What is this universe?
Where is it?
Why is it?

I am lost and alone.
It is so lonesome and cold.
Where am I?
How am I?
Why am I?

10/4/64

Watching Stars

I am Man on the Earth
        watching Stars.

I am the Earth in the Man
        watching Stars.

I am Earth in the Plant,
I am Plant in the Beast,
I am the Beast in the Man on the Earth
        watching Stars

I am Stardust in the Man.

I am God in the Stardust in the Man on the Earth
        watching Stars.

I am God in the Earth
        watching Stars
            watch the Man on the Earth
                watching Stars.

I am God in the Earth watching
        Stars watch
            the Earth
            in the Man
                on the Earth
                    watching Stars.

1988

"Science is not only compatible with spirituality; it is a profound source of spirituality."

Carl Sagan

As Inside, So Outside; As Above, So Below

Acknowledgements

I wish to thank the following people whose efforts and support contributed to the birthing of this book.

Robin Bloor and Karnak Press for believing that this material offers a meaningful contribution to the possibility of a new relationship between science and the Perennial Wisdom.

Federico Balsa, my enthusiastic and most helpful friend and editor, for not only improving the text and flow of the material but for his encouragement and support when doubt would creep into my efforts.

Ines Dansey, Jack Clark, Stephen Grant, and Richard Webb, for their support as sounding boards for my ideas and writing style.

Joan Dow, my creative producer, marketing maven and a relentless bringer of humor and excitement to the project.

Jeff Zeleski, Editor of *Parabola Magazine*, for his interest in helping my writing find an audience.

Bonnie Phillips and Fifth Press, Salt Lake City, Utah, for granting permission to reuse portions of the *Introduction* I authored for Keith Buzzell's last book, *The Third Striving*, 2014 Fifth Press

Marlena Buzzell for her deep friendship and permission to reprint a quote from *The Neurophysiology of Television Viewing: a Preliminary Report,* Keith A. Buzzell, DO, unpublished manuscript.

My Companions in the study of Gurdjieff's Fourth Way for all their help, intentional and inadvertent, in causing me to see myself with a depth of honesty and acceptance that inspired and informed my understanding in a way rarely possible in ordinary life.

George Ivanovich Gurdjieff and all his students for the help and guidance that opened for me the doorway to a world I could never have imagined.

As Inside, So Outside; As Above, So Below

The Author

Stephen Aronson is a psychotherapist, now retired, after forty years of practice, with an eclectic background ranging from cognitive behavioral therapy to the alchemical approach of Carl Jung.

His spiritual life has been a search for verification of a deeper reality underlying the ordinary world of our senses.

His personal aim has been to find a reconciliation between science and spirituality which would also allow reconciling the concept of Universal intelligence with rationality.

After a dozen years in Jungian analysis and four decades of study and practice in the system of transformational psychology introduced to the West by G. I. Gurdjieff, he has sought to find an approach to illustrate these deep and complex ideas and methods in common language and universally shared experiences. He believes the arcane language of specialized methods, although necessary for advanced training, is often a barrier for those seeking an initial understanding.

He received a B.S. from Penn State University in 1965 and an M.A. and PhD in clinical psychology from the University of Connecticut in 1970. After initially teaching at Arizona State and Alfred University, he left academia to pursue immersion in clinical practice.

He co-authored a pioneering book on the management of stress, *The Stress Management Workbook: An Action Plan for Taking Control of Your Life and Health,* Appleton-Century-Croft, 1981, with physician Michael Mascia.

In 2022 he released *The Search for Meaning and the Mystery of Consciousness: A Psychologist's Journey through Gurdjieff and Jung.*

He has published on the contributions of G. I. Gurdjieff in the *Proceedings* of the annual *All and Everything International Humanities Conference,* and *Parabola,* a magazine dedicated to Myth, Tradition and Search for Meaning.

Steve lives in rural Maine where he retired in 2013.

As Inside, So Outside; As Above, So Below

Publications by Stephen Aronson

Papers

Preparation for the Third Line of Work: Threading the Needle Between Wiseacring and the Law of Hazard,
Proceedings of the All and Everything International Humanities Conference, 2009

Egoism and Compassion: A Higher Perspective,
Proceedings of the All and Everything International Humanities Conference, 2010

Divided Attention and the Search for Self,
Proceedings of the All and Everything International Humanities Conference, 2014

Enneagram Perspectives: The Enneagram as a Multidimensional Symbol,
Proceedings of the All and Everything International Humanities Conference, 2018

Bodies – Higher and Lower,
Proceedings of the All and Everything International Humanities Conference, *2021*

Group Dynamics and the Future of Gurdjieff Groups,
Proceedings of the All and Everything International Humanities Conference, 2024

Articles

The Golden Rule and the Transformation of Being, Parabola Magazine, NY, Winter, 2021-22

Starlight, Parabola Magazine, NY, Winter, Summer, 2023

Books

The Search for Meaning and the Mystery of Consciousness: A Psychologist's Journey Through Gurdjieff and Jung, The Karnak Press, Austin, Texas, 2022

As Inside, So Outside: As Above, So, Below: Reconciling Science and Spirituality Through Consciousness, The Karnak Press, Austin, Texas, 2024

The Stress Management Workbook: An Action Plan for Taking Control of Your Life and Health, Appleton-Century Croft, NY, 1979

The First Book in this Series

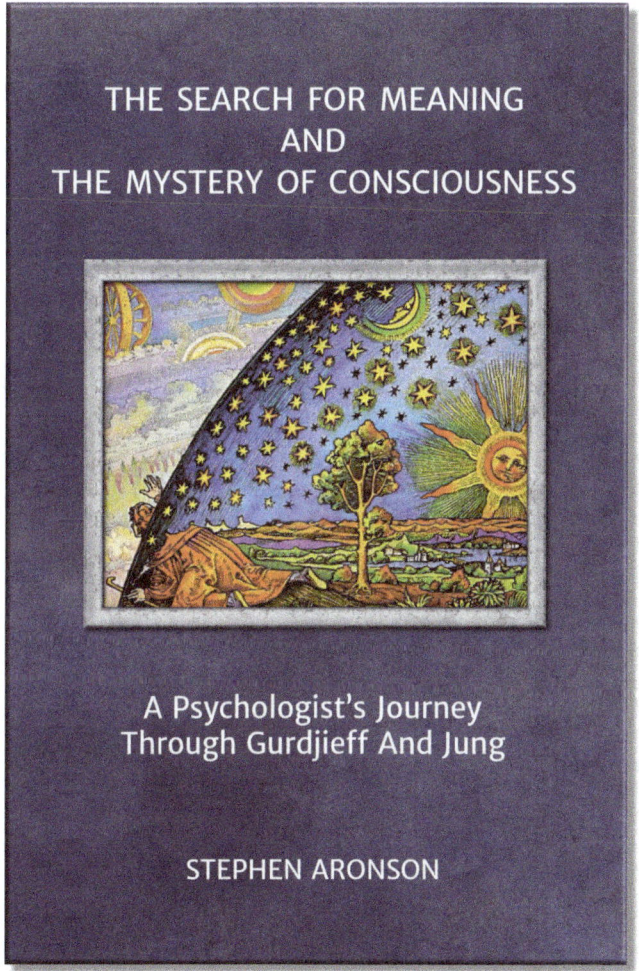

THE SEARCH FOR MEANING
AND
THE MYSTERY OF CONSCIOUSNESS

A Psychologist's Journey
Through Gurdjieff And Jung

STEPHEN ARONSON

Available from Amazon
and other web-based book stores